N. B. (Nicholas Belfield) Dennys

The China review

Notes and queries on the Far East

N. B. (Nicholas Belfield) Dennys

The China review
Notes and queries on the Far East

ISBN/EAN: 9783741169304

Manufactured in Europe, USA, Canada, Australia, Japa

Cover: Foto ©Andreas Hilbeck / pixelio.de

Manufactured and distributed by brebook publishing software
(www.brebook.com)

N. B. (Nicholas Belfield) Dennys

The China review

The connection of the present Editor with the *China Review* ceases with this Number, and it will in future be conducted by the Proprietor, with very competent assistance on the part of resident Sinologues. In severing his connection with a periodical, which, he trusts he may say, has achieved a creditable reputation in the literary circles of Hongkong and China, the retiring Editor would bespeak for its future conductors the same cordial support as has hitherto been accorded to it.

CONTENTS OF No. 3.

		Page.
The Folk-lore of China, (*Continued from page* 84)		139
The Chinese Vernaculars,	By C. F. PRESTON	152
Trip to the City of Leen Chau,	C. F. PRESTON	160
Legend of the Building of Peking,	G. C. STENT	168
Chinese Explorations of the Indian Ocean During the Fifteenth Century, (*Continued from Vol. III.*, *page* 67)	W. F. MAYERS	173
An Introduction to A Retrospect of Forty Years of Foreign Intercourse with China,	G. NYE	191
Short Notices of New Books and Literary Intelligence,		200
Notes and Queries on Eastern Matters:—		
Chinese Jessamine,	H. F. H.	203
Torture in British and Chinese Prisons,		203
Fusang,		204
Bells,	H. A. B.	204
Red as a Festive Colour,	ETHNOLOGIST	205
The Natural History of China,	NATURALIST	205
Books Wanted, Exchanges, &c.,		205

THE CHINA REVIEW.

THE FOLK-LORE OF CHINA.

(Continued from page 84.)

VI.—SUPERSTITIONS AS TO VARIOUS SUBJECTS.

There are in China a large number of generally believed Superstitions which it is difficult to class under any of the foregoing heads. The mysterious properties ascribed to the hare are peculiarly interesting. A prejudice against eating its flesh is coeval with Chinese history. In the Erh-ya* we find it stated that the people of Yo-yang "considered the hare to be a telluric genius so that nobody dared to hunt it," and throughout China it has always been looked upon (especially the red variety) as a divine animal.† Albino hares are regarded as omens of good, and their appearance a mark of heavenly approval. In Dr. Eitel's *Handbook of Chinese Buddhism*, Art. *Sakchi*, we read, that an unselfish hare who threw itself into the fire, to offer its flesh as food for others, was transferred by Indra to the centre of the Moon.‡ The superstition concerning hares is common to China and India. Nor, though it does not take precisely the same form, is a belief in the portentous attributes of this animal wanting at home. For a hare to cross a man's path early in the morning is an ill omen throughout

Europe. And a Highlander of the 42nd Regiment, in his printed memoirs, notices the same harbinger of evil as having crossed his own path on a day of personal disaster in Spain.* It is noteworthy that the Goddess Freya is represented as attended by hares, who act as train and light-bearers. The hare moreover is reputed to be one of the commonest disguises of a witch in all the Northern Countries of Europe.†

Equally as widespread as the foregoing superstition is a common belief, that drowned bodies may be discovered by throwing into the water certain objects which, it is asserted, will stop over the exact spot where the corpse may lie. The American Indians use a chip of cedar wood. In England a loaf of bread loaded with quicksilver is used, while in Ireland similar use is made of a wisp of straw, bound round with a strip of parchment on which some cabalistic words have been written by the parish priest. In Java, and in some parts of China, a living goat (a sheep, I believe, will do as well) is cast into the water, and its dead body will, as is believed, indicate the resting place of the drowned man. As regards running streams it is easy to account for this com-

爾 雅.
† N. & Q. C. & J., Vol. II., p. 69.
‡ *Handbook of Chinese Buddhism*, p. 107.

* *Predictions Realised*, p. 87.
† *Folk-lore of the Northern Counties*, p. 166 *et seq.*

mon superstition by natural facts, but the varied forms it assumes are interesting. Another Chinese superstition relates to the use of salt, which is thrown into the water when any one has been rescued from drowning. A few months since a correspondent wrote to a Shanghai newspaper as follows:—" Yesterday afternoon a youngster of the Chinese nationality fell into the water off a pontoon. So his relatives set to work to fish him out, which humane act being accomplished, was followed by two old women very properly pulling his ears for trying to drown himself, and giving them trouble, while another old woman threw salt into the water at the spot he had fallen in. Can any of your readers inform me what the salt-throwing meant, and whether it is a custom on such occasions to do so?" The query remained unanswered. Nor has subsequent enquiry enabled me to throw any light upon the subject. "It's a local custom," was the only answer I could get. But a reference to Brand gives us some very interesting facts in connection with the use of salt for the purposes of lustration.* Flinging salt over the left shoulder to avert threatened calamity is a well-known custom. The Greeks and Romans used it in their lustrations, and Jews and Pagans alike used it in their sacrifices as a propitiation. The Romans especially designed it as a propitiatory offering to avert the vengeance of Stygian or infernal Gods—an exact parallel to the Chinese custom. In the Isle of Man, a gift of salt is an essential element in numerous transactions. The Scotch used to, and perhaps still, put salt in the first milk taken from a cow after calving. That the Chinese should also credit salt with propitiatory virtues also is therefore curious. Another item of our own household folk-lore, concerning the last piece of any edible left on a dish, is purely Chinese. While our goodwives give it the name of the "bachelor's bit," the Chinese call it the "poison piece,"—not because it is in itself poisonous, but because he who

* *Pop. Antiquities*, Vol. III., p. 160 *et. seq.*

takes it may fare as badly as if he had been veritably poisoned. The Chinese think it unlucky to have the spout of a kettle, standing on the fire, turned outwards;—a belief I can only match by our superstition that it forebodes ill to cross two knives on the dinner table, being unable to trace the origin of either superstition.

I can hardly avoid in this place a notice of the singular geomantic superstitions known as *Fêng shui*, regarding which Dr. Eitel has written so excellent a brochure. That learned writer answers the question "what is Fêng-shui?" in the following words: "Fêng-shui [the words themselves signify wind and water] is, as I take it, but another name for natural science. . . . It is simply the blind gropings of the Chinese mind after a system of natural science, which gropings, untutored by practical observation of nature, and trusting almost exclusively in the truth of alleged ancient tradition, and in the force of abstract reasoning, naturally left the Chinese mind completely in the dark." No more accurate definition for scientific purposes could be given, and to those who feel an interest in the subject I cannot do better than recommend the perusal of his work. But for present purposes, in which the practical rather than theoretical side of popular belief is necessarily dealt with, the reply must be framed somewhat differently. Fêng-shui, then, is a system of geomancy which determines the good or ill luck of localities as regards their occupation for purposes of building, cultivation, burial, etc., etc. By way of illustrating this interpretation the following paragraph from a Shanghai newspaper, written of course simply for "news" purposes, is apposite—"The general excitement caused in Hangchow, in common, apparently, with the rest of the province, was some weeks ago intensified by a development of the well-known superstition of *Fêng-shui*. A number of people having died in a certain part of the town, enquiries began to be made as to the cause of a mortality somewhat specially localised. But instead of looking, as Westerns almost instinctively would, to the physical conditions and environments of the district, the good folks of Hangchow called in the learning of the geomancers to explain the cause of the 'evil influence.' These worthies were not long in pointing to a range of buildings belonging to one of the American Missions, that stood on a hill overlooking the district where the abnormal mortality had prevailed. These buildings, though not high 'in themselves, were yet elevated by their site above all the surrounding buildings, and thus they interrupted the benign influences of the *Fêng-shui*. The question then came to be, how the evil was to be remedied. The traditional mode of procedure would have been to organise a mob, raise a disturbance, and during its continuance contrive to pull down or burn the obnoxious premises. But, on the one hand, past experience of foreigners has convinced the authorities that this way of dealing with foreign property is sure to entail serious consequences ; while on the other, the satisfactory results of diplomatic action as illustrated at Peking has gradually inclined them to the *suaviter-in-modo* policy. Accordingly a number of the gentry were commissioned to proceed to Ningpo and put themselves in communication with the United States Consul on the subject. Arrived in Ningpo they drew up a petition to that gentleman, setting forth the fears and anxieties which were excited among the common people of Hangchow, by the disturbance of the *Fêng-shui* occasioned by the mission premises in question, and setting forth the willingness of the authorities to grant them a site and erect buildings on some other site to be agreed on between them and the missionaries, or to pay the missionaries a money equivalent for the surrender of their property. The missionaries, on being communicated with by Dr Lord, signified their preference of the proposal to grant them an equally eligible site and erect suitable buildings elsewhere, in

exchange for their existing property, and this arrangement is now in course of being carried out." No better instance of the difficulties which Fêng-shui presents to foreign missionary and commercial enterprise could be adduced.

A superstitious belief in the value of human blood and portions of the body as medicinal aids seems to be common to the ignorant classes of many nations. Just two years ago, a number of lepers were reported to have made their appearance at Whampoa and its vicinity, attacking and killing healthy men, that they might drink the blood and eat the intestines of those killed, which, lepers are under the firm belief, will cure them of their loathsome disease. The native residents at Whampoa became very apprehensive about this, and exercised very great caution in their trips into the surrounding country in obedience to the time-honoured custom of worshipping at the tombs. A Chinaman, who was employed on board one of the river steamers, caught the disease, and, as was currently stated at the time, resorted to the *modus operandi* stated above. Female lepers, by the way, believe that they will become free from the disease if they communicate it to men willing to live with them, and as some are always to be found sufficiently dead to ordinary feeling to do so, leprosy has by this means been spread more than it would otherwise be.

The idea of cannibalism for other purposes is by no means unfamiliar to the Cantonese. When the rebels, called "patriots" by the half-informed enthusiasts of those days, held possession of the Blenheim Reach Fort, they used to drink the blood and eat the hearts of the Imps, (*i.e.* foreigners) whom they made prisoners. Colonel Yule, in his exhaustive work on Marco Polo (Vol. I., p. 275), devotes a lengthy note to the subject of Chinese and Tibetan cannibalism. The Arab travellers of the 9th century relate that, "In China it occurs sometimes that the governor of a province revolts from his duty to the emperor. In such a case he is slaughtered and eaten. In fact the Chinese eat the flesh of all men who are executed by the sword." Dr. Rennie states (and I can myself confirm the assertion) that after an execution at Peking certain large pith-balls are steeped in the blood of the defunct criminal, and under the name of "blood-bread" are sold as a medicine for consumption. It is only to the blood of decapitated criminals that any such healing power is attributed. "It is asserted that the executioners of Mr. de Chappedelaine, a Romish missionary murdered in Yunnan in 1862, were seen to eat the heart of their victim, and Mr. Cooper, the well-known traveller, was told by a Bishop of the same mission, that he had seen men in Yunnan eating the heart and brains of a celebrated robber, who had been executed." In all these cases the idea underlying this horrible act is, that by eating a portion of the victim, especially the heart, one acquires the valour with which he was endowed.

Nor do the Chinese stand alone in their silly stories respecting the use of the children's eyes and blood for photographic purposes. I note that a recent report of the Smyrna mission alludes to a superstition amongst the Greek Christians of the Levant curiously similar. They hold that the Jewish ritual enjoins the shedding of blood at the feast of the Passover, and that the Jews annually inveigle a Christian child into their toils, fatten it up, and then open its arteries to utilize the blood.* This blood, it is believed, is kneaded into the unleavened bread

* Alexander, if we may credit the account given by Quintus Curtius, was terrified by blood flowing from inside his soldiers' bread during the siege of Tyre in 332 B. C. His seer, Aristauda, foresaw in this crimson efflux of the vital stream out of the commissariat a happy issue for the Macedonian; and the warriors thus never took Tyre. From the year 1001, the alarming spectacle of the bleeding host and bread, as well as the bewitched bloody milk, several times in each century, gave simple folk a scare. But the victims of superstition have the bump of casualty remarkably developed, and, in 1410, thirty-eight Jews were burnt to ashes because they had tortured the consecrated host until it bled.—*Chambers' Journal.*

by the priests, who afterwards distribute this devilish confectionery to their congregations, for a small pecuniary consideration.*

But the superstitions regarding the uses of human blood or flesh are not confined to the instances above given. It used to be believed at Canton, and perhaps now is, that the blood of an unborn infant was all effective for magical purposes.† It is used as a charm against husbands by a sect called 迷夫教, a set of young unmarried women, comprising a sisterhood who are sworn never to marry. If forced by their parents to do so, they then employ this charm to destroy their husbands in order to remain single and be faithful to the oaths of the sisterhood. A case is on record in which a Fokienese availed himself of this drug to influence a woman for improper purposes, and her subsequent death in child-birth was regarded as the natural result of her yielding to the horrible charm.

More wide-spread is a belief in the restorative qualities of human flesh and

* The object of the ceremony is, according to the myth, to cleanse the Jewish race in general, and the participators of the rite in particular, from the guilt of Calvary. It does not appear that the Chinese Jews have any legend of similar import.

† A correspondent of *Notes and Queries* writes: "Wife-beating, to the effusion of blood, may be a novel method of securing luck in herring-fishery, but to draw blood is practised in some of the fishing villages on the north-east coast of Scotland, under the belief that success follows the act. The act must be performed on New Year's day, and the fortune is his only who is the first to shed blood. If the morning of the New Year is such as to allow the boats of the village to put to sea, there is quite a struggle as to which boat will reach the ground first, so as to gain the coveted prize, the first to shed blood of the year. If the weather is unfavorable for fishing, those in possession of guns—and a great many of the fishermen's houses possess one—are out, gun in hand, along the shore, before daybreak, in search of some bird or wild animal, no matter how small, that they may draw blood, and thus make sure of one year's good fortune." Mr. Latouche in his *Travels in Portugal* (1875) narrates a story illustrative of the national belief in the wehr wolf (lobis-homem), in which a Portuguese "wise woman" is reported as saying that "if a *lobis homem* can murder and drink the blood of a newly born child, the enchantment ceases and she is a lobis-homem no longer."

blood to the siek. Parents suffering from long standing or dangerous diseases are frequently offered a decoction of medicine in which is mixed a piece of the flesh of one of their children. It is considered an act of great filial piety to cut a slice off one's calf to mix it with medicine for a parent. The practice is still followed even to the present day. Honourable mention is often made in the *Peking Gazette* of such cases. It has of late been written down by the native press, particulary by the *Chinese Mail*. A recent issue of the Shanghai *Courier and Gazette* (November 1875) contained the following paragraph amongst it local items:—" Two model sons are now living at Soochow, whose mother was one day taken alarmingly ill. They were very poor; but medical assistance was urgently necessary, and so the elder brother went to implore the assistance of a celebrated doctor. He was only able, of course, to offer the great man a small fee; and the great man loftily refused to come. The poor lad threw himself on the ground before him and bumped his head till it ached, but the doctor was quite immoveable. So he went home and told his younger brother how unsuccessful he had been. The unfortunate woman was dying; what was to be done? At length the young boy hit upon an expedient. He cut a great piece of flesh out of his left arm, boiled it down to a broth, and gave it his mother to drink. It is said that she recovered." In May 1874, a memorial in the *Peking Gazette* records how the Deputy Governor of Honan petitioned in reference to a dutiful daughter who cut a piece of flesh from her arm, in order to cure her father of his sickness. "In the present Holy Dynasty, filial piety rules the Empire, and this doctrine originates in the female sex. In the district of Chinyang there lived a daughter remarkable for her filial piety, whose name after her marriage, was Mrs. Wang. In the fifth year of the reign of the Emperor Heen-fung, this young lady's father became dangerously ill,

and his filial daughter, lighting incense sticks, announced (to the gods) her desire to sacrifice her own body for her father's sake. After this announcement, her father's illness increasing, and his physicians being unable to cure him, this filial daughter secretly cut off a piece of flesh from her arm, and putting it into the medicine prescribed, gave it to her father who, on eating it, immediately recovered. Some time afterwards the daughter's female attendants, perceiving the mark on her arm, questioned her as to the cause and learned from her the facts already stated. There was not a single individual of all those who heard the narrative who was not struck with amazement." The young lady in question was shortly afterwards married, but her father dying some ten years afterwards she "pined away and died for grief." The petition from which the above quotation is made prays the Emperor to order that a Triumphal Arch be erected to her memory, as was usual in cases when extreme filial piety had been displayed, and the petition was of course granted.

A common saying that "a selfish child will be cut while being shaved" embodies an idea not altogether unfamiliar to ourselves. But another Chinese superstition, which certainly existed in full force at one time, though I have failed to get any positive confirmation of its existence at the present day, obliges us to seek its parallel amongst other than Aryan races. A belief in weather conjuring by means of "rain stones" seems to have been introduced into China from Mongolia, and though it never took extensive root it attracted sufficient attention to induce the Emperor Shih-tsung in 1724-25, to issue an edict on the subject. It is addressed to the Mongolian Banner Corps, and says: "If I offering prayer in sincerity have yet room to fear it may please Heaven to have *my* prayer unanswered, it is truly intolerable that mere common people wishing for rain should at their own caprice set up altars of earth, and bring together a rabble of Hoshang and Taossü to conjure the spirits to gratify their wishes." Colonel Yule, in his *Marco Polo*, from which (I. p. 273) I take this reference, gives some long and interesting notes on the subject. Rain stones are used by the Samoans in the Pacific, and if my memory does not deceive me, by some of the North American Indian tribes also.

A popular belief exists in Central China that the practice of gymnastics, if carried out with sufficient faithfulness, will enable the student to avoid the common lot, and pass bodily into a future state "ascending to heaven with his fleshly body." That such a belief exists is not unlikely, and it is probably a vulgar superstition based on the more reasonable opinion that such exercises tend to extreme longevity. Another queer superstition (the adjective is not classical but expressive) relates to bridges. I have already adverted to the care taken as regards houses by placing on them charms, &c., to avert possible evil. But bridges, for some mysterious reason, have occult virtues and defects of their own. A native account says, "If bridges are not placed in proper positions such as the laws of geomancy indicate they may endanger the lives of thousands by bringing about a visitation of small-pox or sore eyes (!). They materially affect the prosperity of the neighbourhood. There is a legend that during the building of the stone bridge situated near the small eastern gate of Shanghai 陸家百橋 (the 'Luh-family bridge,') some difficulty was found in laying the foundations. The builder thereupon vowed to Heaven the lives of two thousand children if the stones could be placed properly. The Goddess addressed, however, intimated that she would not require all their lives, but that the number in question would be attacked by small pox. This took place, and about half of those attacked died." Stories like this circulated amongst coolies and compradores are a fair specimen of popular legendry in this connection. But why bridges should especially require such sacrifices it is difficult to say.

Amongst what may be termed domestic superstitions is one that, if a person be afflicted with a swelling, touching it three times with the hem of a woman's garment is efficacious as a cure. If, when one is boiling a pot full of liquid, a straw be tied round the neck of the pot, it is believed that the contents will never boil over or get burned. Another piece of cook's folk-lore relates to eggs. As everybody knows an egg suddenly plunged into boiling water will most likely break. But the Chinese cook averts this occurrence by previously describing a circle with the egg round the rim of the pot, which he believes is an infallible protection against any fracture of the shell. The Japanese, by the way, draw auguries from the noise made by boiling. Over a bright fire, a rice boiler is said to vibrate with such violence at times as to give forth a loud humming noise. If this begins faintly and grows afterwards stronger it is said to indicate good luck; if loudly, the reverse is predicted, but in such cases it should at once be stopped by enveloping it in the under-clothing of a female (a virgin, if possible.)

A curious antidote against sickness is very commonly applied by parents at Canton to their infant children on the fifth day of the fifth month. This consists in staining their foreheads and navels with cinnabar or vermilion, leaves of the sago palm and garlic bulbs being at the same time suspended over the entrance doors to prevent the intrusion of evil spirits. A medicated cake prepared at *noon* of the day in question, and known as "the noon day tea" (午時茶) is also in much repute for the cure of diseases, as is also a sort of congee boiled at the same hour with five kinds of pease.

The all-pervading *yang* and *yin* principle so naturally influences the whole arcana of Chinese belief that it is not surprising to find it applied to the care of such useful contributors to the national industries as silkworms. These are said to belong to the *yang* or male influence and to be under the protection of a special constellation. Anything male, such as men, sunlight, &c., is congenial to them, and anything female deleterious. Hence pregnant women (development of the *yin* principle) are not allowed to approach them; and even the presence of a new-born child in too close proximity is thought to be deleterious.

Finally I may note that a curious superstition obtains regarding murderers. It is believed that if the corpse of the murdered man lies with its fists closed, it is a sign that the murderer will soon be captured. If on the contrary the hands are extended, the omen foretells that he will for at least some time make good his escape. It is strange, by the way, that so widespread a belief as that relating to the bleeding of a corpse when touched by its murderer has not some analogy in China. At least I have failed to find any, though a not quite dissimilar superstitious idea is prevalent, that if a man has died a violent death—either by process of the law, or by the act of a murderer—and the dead man is dissatisfied, blood will come out of his mouth, eyes and nostrils on the appearance of a close relative.

VII.—GHOSTS, APPARITIONS, AND SUPERNATURAL BEINGS.*

No one who has thus far followed my imperfect efforts to convey an idea of the popular beliefs of the Chinese will be surprised to find that ghosts and apparitions occupy an even greater place in their superstitious lore than is the case with ourselves. In the words of a native friend, "China is full of ghosts." There is scarcely a popular play in which a ghost does not play a conspicuous part in aiding to right the wronged or to punish the guilty. The person to whom

* In the compilation of this and the following chapter I must express my great obligations to Mr. C. T. Gardner, of H. M. Consular service, Canton, to the Rev. J. Chalmers, M.A., and to Mr. Chun Ayin, of the *Chinese Mail*, for manuscript notes which they have kindly placed at my disposal. I have also quoted freely from an amusing paper published in the *Daily Press* entitled "Bogey in the Middle Kingdom," and from a contribution which appeared some time since in the Shanghai *Courier* newspaper over the signature " Liu."

he appears on such occasions generally counterfeits either sleep or insensibility; but now and then while wakeful and active the actor (especially if he be the ruffian of the piece) is scared out of his senses by the apparition in the most approved melodramic style. Many popular stories turn also on the appearance of supposed ghosts, who turn out to be quite *bonâ fide* citizens in the flesh and simply enforce the moral that conscience makes a coward of the wrongdoer. A story of this sort runs to the following effect, and narrates an incident stated by Mr. C. T. Gardner to have happened only some five years ago at Chinkeang. There were two partners, named Chang and Li, on one occasion returning by way of the canal from Yangchow, where they had been collecting debts. Chang saw Li standing on the edge of the boat, and the crime of pushing him into the water, and thus becoming sole possessor of the money, suggested itself. Chang, therefore, pushed Li into the canal. Next year, at the time the murder was committed, Chang fell very ill, and the ghost of Li appeared to him in a threatening form, and told him that unless he paid over the sum properly belonging to the dead man's family, he would die. Chang promised to do so, and got well, but his health being restored he broke his promise, and still kept the money. Again, the following year, at the same time, Li's ghost again appeared, looking still angrier. Again Chang was induced to make the promise, and this time he kept it. However, his health seemed permanently to suffer, everything went wrong, business fell off, and he determined to try and change his luck by migrating to other parts; he consequently went to Honan. What was his astonishment when he again saw Li, not now in the middle of the night by the side of the bed where he lay sick, but in broad daylight, and in the street. His terror was extreme, he rushed forward, and made a ko-tow, and said, "I have already done as you ordered me, why do you still haunt me?" To which Li replied, "I am no ghost; what do you mean?"

Then Chang told him how he had twice appeared, and how his share of the money had been paid to his family. Li then said, "So, it was not an accident my falling into the river? I had neglected to pay due respect to the spirit of my father, and when I tumbled in the river, and was nearly drowned, I thought it a punishment for my impiety."

"The spirits of the dead," remarks Mr. Chalmers, "were perhaps known at first only as objects of superstitious fear under the name Kwei 鬼 ghosts. The top of this character is supposed to represent a human skull. It had from the first an unpleasant association, and hence it is seldom used in speaking respectfully of the dead. In the poetry it occurs only twice, once as our modern Ghost, and once as the name of a place —Ghostland.

"An interesting statement is attributed to Confucius in the Book of Rites (§ Tan-kung) that in the time of the Hea, the earliest dynasty, they did not sacrifice to the dead, but simply made for them incomplete implements of bamboo, earthenware without polish, harps unstrung, organs untuned, and bells unhung, which they called 'bright implements' implying that the dead are spirits (shen) and bright. There is something really beautiful in this; and the substitution of 'bright spirits' or 'spiritual intelligences' for 'ghosts' is an euphemism of which we feel the necessity as much as the Chinese; for who likes to speak of his relations as gone to the shades and to the fellowship of ghosts?"

One peculiarity of the Chinese belief respecting ghosts is forcibly recalled by Charles Dickens's description of the Ghost of Christmas Past in his famous "Carol." They are frequently seen in shapeless form, i.e. that the head will first be visible and then the feet, then the body, and so on, the various parts appearing and disappearing in swift succession. Another quaint belief is that a ghost has no chin, and to say to a Cantonese "ni mo ha-pa"—"You've no chin," is equivalent to saying "You're

a Ghost." Furthermore, the conventional white clothing which European superstition bestows on nearly all ghostly visitors is absent from the Chinese idea. A ghost in this country always appears in the dress he was accustomed to wear during life—a very Marley in fact—and conducts himself in a very ordinary way. There is indeed a refreshing absence of the fee-faw-fum element in Chinese ghostology, this eminently practical people taking a most matter-of-fact view of spirit vagaries. They agree with us however in allotting the hours of darkness to such visitors, who, as with ourselves, are compelled to disappear as the cock's crow announces the returning dawn. The candle flame which with us burns blue as the being from another world intrudes himself, is in China alleged to burn green—an odd reminder of the "green fear" of the Greeks. Most Chinese ghost stories turn upon some end to be accomplished by the supernatural visitor; they retail none of the sprightly friskiness attributed to ghosts in Western lands, and altogether the Chinese specimen presents, as a rule, an edifying illustration of how to do one's work in the quietest and most straightforward manner possible. It must not however be supposed that they are endowed by popular belief with benevolent intentions. On the contrary they are supposed to be maliciously inclined, and the very fact that the words for "ghost" and "devil" are the same, and form a portion of the objectionable epithets applied to foreigners (Kwei-tsze in mandarin or Fan-kwai in Cantonese) demonstrates the popular belief. To see a ghost is almost always regarded as an evil omen, and a Chinaman is quite as easily scared as a European by the unwelcome sight. One thus visited is described by his pitying neighbours as "down in his luck." As a rule, ghosts in China, it is alleged, most often appear either to intimate friends or relations or to downright enemies. In the former case it is to request the fulfilment of some unaccomplished duty or to aid virtue in distress, when the ghost gives the weaker but upright party material aid in disposing of his antagonist. As an illustration of the first-named sort of apparition, I quote the following recently communicated by a resident to the *North China Daily News*, as told him by his teacher to excuse his non-appearance for some few days:—

"It happened thus; three years ago a soldier who lived near our house was ordered to join his regiment, which was about to march against the rebels. As he was going to battle he did not wish to take his money with him, and he called on my uncle and asked him to take charge of $40, the amount of his property, until his return. My uncle accordingly took charge of the money, and the soldier joined his regiment; but he must have been killed in battle, as we have never heard from him since.

"The day before yesterday, my uncle, who has for some time been suffering from illness, called us to his bedside, and told us that he was about to die. The soldier, he said, had appeared to him and insisted that my uncle should immediately join him in Hades. We asked my uncle whether he had committed any fault with regard to the $40, for which we might make some atonement by punishing him in any way? He replied that the money was all right, and that we should find it in a certain drawer which he pointed out. My uncle died that day, and it was of course impossible, under such circumstances, that I could come to your Excellency's place to study."

Among recent stories of ghosts is one related in a native newspaper of a mandarin who met his death in the late collision between the *Fusing* and *Ocean*. The unfortunate man was a passenger in the Chinese steamer *Fusing*, which was sunk in the catastrophe, over 60 other people being also drowned. According to the story his ghost appeared to his wife, who was living in Soochow, streaming with water from head to foot. He told her that he had unfortunately been drowned and could therefore enjoy no more of her society.

He also stated that he had sent by a certain friend of his some money for her use before he took passage in the *Fusing*, and that the friend would arrive shortly. The wife was left in a state of bewilderment, and did not exactly know what to make of it. A day or two afterwards the friend named actually came with the packet of dollars, his arrival being shortly followed by the intelligence of the *Fusing's* disaster.

Another story relates to a young Cantonese, who was made commander of a Chinese man-of-war belonging to the Foochow Arsenal fleet. Shortly after his promotion, he was taken ill and died. He was unmarried as he was very young—only 23 years of age. When he fell sick, he was living at the house of a very intimate friend, a compradore in one of the foreign firms at Foochow. After his death, the friend frequently saw his ghost, and one night he saw it more distinctly than ever. He was lying in bed half asleep and half awake, when he saw the ghost standing by his bedside weeping. The friend addressed it and said: "Young man, you need not cry, it is your fate; you should be satisfied with it." Thereupon the ghost disappeared, and never shewed itself again to the same party. The ghost showed itself however to the men on board the ship he had been commanding, being often seen to pace up and down the deck, as was his wont at night during his lifetime, and sometimes place itself in the attitude of drilling the men. Though the appearance here narrated seems to have been objectless, the story is quoted as being the type of numberless others which find insertion in the native prints.

The Chinese endow certain sorts of ghosts with peculiarly malevolent powers. Thus those of women who die in childbed, or while pregnant, are peculiarly obnoxious, and those of suicides still more so. The ghosts of those who die natural deaths seldom appear to the survivors; as a rule the fact of a man's ghost appearing implies that he has died by violence.* The commonest type of ghost story to be met with in China is that wherein somebody who has been foully dealt with appeals to those who represent his interests to avenge him. It would of course be more odd if there were no coincidences pointing to the truth of the alleged appearances than if there were not. But I must confess that in China as elsewhere they sometimes leave a *bona fide* impression of the marvellous which can neither be explained nor rejected.

When a man has been murdered by another, his ghost will, it is believed, haunt the murderer wherever he goes, and will only be prevented from doing him a mischief by the want of a suitable opportunity. Thus the presence of idols in the same room completely neutralizes the ghost's power, and it is moreover believed that in any case no vital injury can be inflicted on the guilty party until the time of his death, as recorded in the Book of Fate, has arrived. The ghosts of suicides (who are distinguished by wearing red silk handkerchiefs) haunt the places in which they committed the fatal deed and endeavour to persuade others to follow their example; at times, it is believed, even attempting to play executioner by strangling those who reject their advances. Mr Gardner

* Lady Fanshaw, visiting the head of an Irish sept in his moated baronial grange, was made aware that banshees are not peculiar to Scotland. Awakened at midnight by an awful, unearthly scream, she beheld by the light of the moon a female form at the window of her room, which was too far from the ground for any woman of mortal mold to reach. The creature owned a pretty, pale face, and red, dishevelled hair, and was clad in the garb of old—very old—Ireland. After exhibiting herself some time, the interesting spectre shrieked twice and vanished. When Lady Fanshaw told her host what she had seen he was not at all surprised. "A near relation," said he, "died last night in this castle. We kept our expectation of the event from you lest it should throw a cloud over the cheerful reception which was your due. Now, before such an event happens in the family and castle, the female spectre you saw always becomes visible. She is believed to be the spirit of a woman of inferior rank, whom one of my ancestors married, *and whom he afterward caused to be drowned in the moat, to expiate the dishonor done to our race.*"—*All the Year Round.*

gives the following story as related to him by a Chinese friend:—"A friend of mine enticed by low rent took a haunted house, and invited a guest to stay with him. My friend declares he had no dread whatever, and that his guest did not even know that the house was haunted. In the middle of the night he heard a noise as if of struggling proceeding from the guest's bed. He went to see what was the matter, and found his friend choking in his sleep. Thinking this might be accidental, he invited three friends to stay with him, and the phenomenon repeated itself on all three at the same time. Frightened at this, he made enquiries, and found a woman had committed suicide in the guest's chamber, and gave up the house." Another story runs as follows:—"Outside the north gate at Hang-chow there was a house haunted by demons, where no human being dared reside, of which the doors were ever barred and locked. A scholar named Ts'ai bought the house: people all told him he was doing a dangerous thing, but he did not heed them. After the deed of sale had been drawn out, none of his family would enter the house. Ts'ai therefore went by himself, and having opened the doors, lit a candle and sat down. In the middle of the night a woman slowly approached with a red silk handkerchief hanging to her neck, and having saluted him, fastened a rope to the beam of the ceiling, and put her neck in the noose. Ts'ai did not in the least change countenance. The woman again fastened a rope and called on Ts'ai to do as she had done, but he only lifted his leg and put his foot in the noose. The woman said 'You're wrong.' Ts'ai laughed, and said, 'On the contrary, it was you who were wrong a long time ago, or else you would not have come to this pass.' The Ghost cried bitterly, and having again bowed to Ts'ai, departed, and from this time the house was no longer haunted. Ts'ai afterwards distinguished himself as a scholar, and some have identified him with Ts'ai-ping-ho, the Provincial Chancellor." A third tale from the same source illustrates what I have called the practical element in Chinese ghost stories: "At Nanchang, in Kiangsi, were two literary men who used to read in the Polar monastery; one was elderly, the other young; they were united by the bonds of closest friendship. The elder one went to his home, and suddenly died. The younger man did not know of it, and went on with his studies at the monastery in the usual way. One night after he had gone to sleep, he saw his old friend open the bed curtains, come to the bed, and put his hand on his shoulder, saying, ' Brother, it is only ten days since I parted from you, and now a sudden sickness has carried me off. I am a Ghost. I cannot however forget our friendship, and so have come to bid adieu.' The young man was so astounded that he could not speak. The old man reassured him, saying, ' If I had wished to injure you why should I have told you I was a Ghost; do not fear then. The reason of my visit is that I have a favor to beg of you with regard to the future.' The young man grew a little calmer, and asked ' What can I do ?' The Ghost replied, 'I have a mother over 70, and a wife not yet 30; a few piculs of rice are needed for their maintenance. I beg you to have mercy upon me, and supply their wants. That is my first request. I have also an essay which I have written, which has not been printed. I beg of you to get a block cut for it, and print it, so that my name may not utterly die out. This is my second request. Next I owe the stationers some thousands of cash, which I have not paid; kindly settle the claim. This is my third request.' The young scholar assented with a nod. The dead man stood up, and said, ' As you have been kind enough to grant my requests, I will depart.' Saying this he was about to go, when the young scholar, who had observed from what he said that there was a great deal of human feeling in him, and also that his appearance was as usual, lost all fear of the Ghost, and tried to detain him, ' We have been such close friends; will you not stay with me now

a little while ?' The dead man wept, and came back and sat on the bed, and having conversed about ordinary topics, again stood up, and said, ' I must now go.' He stood up and did not move, his eyes stared, and gradually his features changed. The young scholar got frightened and said, 'Now you have finished what you had to say, you had better go.' But the dead man stood still, and did not depart. The young man shivered in his bed, and a cold perspiration came over him, but still the guest went not, but stood erect by the bedside. The young man got in a still greater fright, and jumped up and ran away. The Ghost ran with him, and the faster the young man ran, the faster ran the Ghost. After a mile or so of this race they came to a wall, over which the young man vaulted, and fell to the ground. The dead man could not get over the wall, so he hung his head over its ledge, and from his mouth fell some saliva which fell on the young man's face as he lay. At daybreak some passers-by gave the young man some ginger, and he awakened from his trance. Meanwhile the family of the dead man sought the corpse, but could not find it, but when they heard the news of the corpse looking over the wall they took the body and buried it."

Although as I have said there is a general absence of " friskiness " in Chinese ghosts, such pranks as those which have attracted attention at home—throwing down crockery, trampling on the floor, &c.—are not unknown. The only difference is that with us, such annoyances seem usually to be purposeless, while in China they are resorted to attract attention to the ghost's demands. Ghosts, say the natives, are much more liable to appear very shortly after death than at any other period. For the first ten days after the spirit has quitted the body a ghost is said to be 囘 煞 *ui shat* (Canton.), returning to its former haunts and attempting to pursue its ordinary avocations. In such cases it is supposed to be accompanied by celestial police termed Yen-lo-hwang, who are responsible that it duly returns to Hades. In order to discover whether such a visit has been paid, the hall in which the body is laid out is strewn with a smooth layer of sand. If it appears clean, or footmarks only are visible, it may be concluded that the deceased is in a state of happiness; but should the marks of chains or dirt be detected, his fate is supposed to be very much the reverse. I may, by the way, note that to constantly dream of deceased relatives is regarded as a sign that the dreamer will soon die.

The superstitions as to deceased husbands visiting their wives are peculiar, but scarcely calculated for popular explanation. A somewhat contemptuous idea seems to prevail amongst the Chinese regarding the intelligence possessed by ordinary ghosts. They are usually spoken of as stupid and easily amenable to the control of those who remain self-possessed. The ghostly hierarchy is well marked off as to its degrees. Thus, on the 17th of the 7th moon, a ceremony called "appeasing the burning mouths," consists in laying out plates filled with cakes and bearing above them invitations to the "Honourable Homeless Ghosts," or those whose relations being too poor to provide for them, leave them to the tender mercies of the general public. Those are the paupers of Ghostland. The writer already quoted, says in his amusing paper:—"Though the invitations are addressed to Ghosts near and far, there seems to be a sort of poor law which practically confines the relief afforded to Ghosts of the parish. Of course, it is only disreputable Ghosts who thus consent to live on charity. These pauper spirits are said to do a great deal of harm, and cause epidemics, but luckily the firing of crackers is a cure for the diseases thus caused, as it drives the hungry Ghosts elsewhere. Besides these low bred and malevolent hobgoblins, there are aristocratic and benevolent spirits, one of whom rules the destiny of each of the Chinese cities. These Ghosts are called Chêng-hwang, and receive their appoint-

ments in various manners and for various terms. Thus the Chêng-hwang of Chu-chow in Chê-kiang, is the ghost of a man named Shih, who was formerly magistrate of the place, but who died of grief on being unjustly disgraced. He received his appointment from heaven, and appeared to his successor in office to notify the fact. The Chêng-hwang of Hangchow is the ghost of a censor named Chow, who being unjustly sentenced to death, memorialized the throne to slay his only son, as he feared he would rebel to avenge his father. Both were executed, and afterwards it being found out that the accusation was false, the Emperor, to make amends, appointed his ghost Chênghwang of Hangchow in perpetuity, and having executed his accusers, man and wife, made stone images of them, kneeling and in chains, which he caused to be placed in the Chêng-hwang's temple. The Chênghwang of Wu-chang is changed every three to six years, and receives the appointment from the Taoist Patriarch residing at Chang-tien joss-house in Kiangsi, and this is notified to the various Taoist priests."

" The Chinese almanacks describe sixty ' Shin of Offence' or evil ghosts, one of which is abroad on each day of the cycle of sixty. If any one goes out in any particular direction, and afterwards feels heavy-headed or feverish he is supposed to have met this shin. He therefore takes some fruit, rice, &c., and politely bows the creature away in the direction where he met the accident. The shin are pictured in the almanacks as little naked men. When the demons take possession of a sacrificing witch she talks about happiness and misery. Every time they come she is altogether a shin in her eating and drinking and speaking, and every time they go she is altogether a human being. It would be hard to say whether demons are in the witch or the witch in the demons.* "

In an old Chinese farce said to date from the Sung Dynasty entitled 王道士收妖

* Chalmers.

or "How the Taoist priest Wang exorcised the Ghost," Wang goes to a haunted house with all his spiritual apparatus, full robes, mitre, &c., and a gong big enough and noisy enough to frighten the boldest devil. Not a bit however does the ghost quail in the present instance, but seizes the gong, the cap and the robes of the holy man, and vows he will turn the tables. At last the priest goes on his knees, and beseeches the ghost not to exorcise him, as he only came in order to earn a few cash; and had he only known beforehand that his Excellency the ghost was really in the house, he would not have ventured to disturb him. The farce ends by the ghost exorcising the priest.

Ghosts of idols are not unknown to the Chinese. "Ten years ago when the rebels infested the country and the cities were kept under strict restraint, the people of Canton reported that the idol Kwan-yin's *shin*, her body dressed in white and in her hand a yak's tail, perambulated the city wall protecting the rampart; and at San-shuey the common people reported that the rebels saw the *shin* of the idol Hiun-tau, which is outside the South gate, bodily riding on a black tiger and in his hand a golden whip too awful to be meddled with."*

Another case of god-ghosts vissible to the vulgar eye was gravely recorded a few years since in the *Peking Gazette*. When the Mahometans were some time ago besieging the district city of Chang-wei, they suddenly halted, and ran away. The explanation is that when the rebels approached the temple of Ta pi-peh (god of the star Venus) they saw a terrible vision—"gods clad in golden mail and armed with swords and shields, drawn up in battle array, numerous as forest trees, and all along the top of the city wall innumerable red lamps;" and as a general fire of musketry and cannon from the wall was heard, the assailants were scared, and they abandoned their onslaught on the city.

The residence of human ghosts in Hades

* Chalmers.

is supposed to be subject to conditions very like those obtaining amongst mortals. They sally forth on their visits to the world at permitted times and are free so long as they behave themselves. But any infringement of the ghostly laws which regulate their conduct is met by prompt punishment and a seclusion which effectually prohibits their revisiting earthly scenes of pleasure or business. But even when enjoying to the full all the privileges of ghostdom, they are not able at all times to do what they would. Mortals may deter them from appearing by pasting up pictures of Chung-Kwai 鍾葵 the Beelzebub of China, on the walls of their rooms. Talismans written in perfectly unintelligible characters are also in use and, as already seen, Taoist priests are credited with the possession of curious powers as exorcists. Pictures of Warriors pasted on the doors of houses are efficacious, as are also the pieces of perforated paper so often seen on the doors of houses waving from the lintels.

The belief in ghosts does not limit itself to those of mankind only. The spirits of certain animals are also supposed to manifest themselves in a similar way, but this section of the subject will be more fully dealt with under the head of witchcraft and demonology. As an illustration however of animal ghostdom pure and simple, the following story may be cited: A resident at Canton named Ling was the owner of a monkey belonging to a species known as *yuan*, which is supposed to be peculiarly intelligent and possesses an almost human mind. The natives believe that if one of these monkeys has plenty of water given to it, it will attain an enormous size, larger than that of an average man. The monkey in question had been in Mr. Ling's family for some 40 years, but never having been allowed to drink water was of small size. One day Mr. Ling's little son was passing the monkey when it put out its hand and snatched away his cap. The child complained to his father, who thereupon chastised the animal heavily with a whip; upon this the monkey became sulky, refused all food and in a few days died. Shortly afterwards the monkey's ghost began to haunt the house. Food placed on the table vanished mysteriously and many of the curious phenomena attributed to ghostly interference took place. At last a fire broke out in the house unaccountably, and Mr. Ling shifted his residence. But the monkey's ghost still followed him and continued its persecutions. Again he moved house and again the ghost accompanied him, until at length, as a last resource, he took a room in the Temple of the 500 Worthies and finally evaded his persecutor. The monkey ghost did not dare face the gods, and so left him in peace. The party mentioned was but a year ago still residing in the temple.

The foregoing pages, though by no means exhaustive of the subject, will it is thought be sufficient to indicate the agreement of Chinese with Western belief as regards ghosts and apparitions. The line of demarcation between the subjects already treated of, and that of witchcraft and demonology, being somewhat indefinite, those curious in the matter will find additional information in the succeeding chapter under that head.

(*To be continued*).

THE CHINESE VERNACULARS.

A PLEA FOR THE CULTIVATION AND USE OF THE VULGAR TONGUES IN CHINA.

An incident is somewhere related of Washington, that, in sending an order, I think it was through his co-patriot Benj. Franklin, then in France, for a watch, he requested that while little regard should be paid to the ornamentation of the case, particular attention should be given to the interior construction of the works, to the end of keeping correct time. It will not be out of place, at the present time, in view of the preparation for the coming celebration of the centennial anniversary of the Independence of the United States of America, to point to the first citizen president of the Republic, and to the nation which is proud to call him the " Father of his country," as an illustration of the character of modern civilization in special regard to practical ends above every other consideration.

The character of any people in any age finds wonderful expression in its language and literature. By them the state of mental cultivation and moral sentiment may be discovered. They rise and flourish, and fall and revive together. All languages, like living organisms, are all the time changing to meet the exigencies of changing conditions until they die, when they change no more for ever, but are fixed like the fossils in the old geological formations. The dead languages are interesting, not only as containing the records of the past, but what is perhaps of still greater importance they are standards of reference for all coming times. There is no more sure mode of determining the character of any people than by the study of their spoken and written languages which are faithful commentaries on their life. Here all the peculiarities of nation and race, of family and individual, are depicted in true colors. Not knowing the people, a good idea may be obtained from their literature. The terra cotta tablets of ancient Nineveh and Babylon reveal the character of the people. Writings only reveal a part; the common speech is still more important, when it can be examined as a revelation of the facts in question. Much has been said and written about the learning fo the Chinese, but it should not be forgotten that the wealth of literature, as is also the case with the land, houses and goods, belongs to a very small proportion of the people. The great mass of the inhabitants of this empire live in a most deplorable poverty, with but a faint idea and minimum knowledge of books. Many of them have learned a little of the sound, without perceiving any meaning of what they have even committed to memory. The Chinese literature and speech are certainly like the Chinese people. They mutually illustrate and explain each other. They are exceedingly interesting subjects for investigation, the materials for which are most abundant; and when the history comes to be written, it will be found, as all who have paid any attention to the subject know, that all along through the ages there have been cycles of improvement and deterioration in different parts of what is now the Chinese Empire, and there is a striking analogy to be found between China past and present with all other ancient and modern pagan nations.

One point, apropos to the following discussion may be mentioned here; which is that the most ancient of the Chinese classics like those of other nations, as the odes and fragments of historical annals, are in an exceedingly simple style, doubtless in the vulgar tongue of the period in which they were written. The involved and condensed style peculiar to after times is in fact a corruption of ancient simplicity. Modern Chinese literature is not a living child born of conviction and desire to discover and reveal truth, but a dead thing of art, cold as ice, without a breath of life or one warm throb of love for humanity. It is in fact the real expression of cultivated paganism, at the extreme pole opposite to nature reformed by Christianity.

Three centuries ago this subject was of vital importance in the countries of Europe, at the time of the reformation, and it is of equal importance and under very similar conditions, it is believed, to-day in China. It is in the full conviction of this fact that this plea is made, especially directed to Christian missionaries in accordance with the feeling that all real and permanent reform in these Asiatic nations will be accomplished by the spread of the Christian religion; but the subject commends itself to the careful consideration of politicians, to all philanthropists who are praying and waiting for the redemption of the world from all ignorance, crime and misery. It is to be expected that there should be wide differences of opinion in the conclusions drawn from the facts discovered in this comparatively new field of investigation. There is much that is new and peculiar; as great variety in the facts of speech, as in the facts in the different branches of natural science. No two individual existences can be found that are exactly alike, but in the midst of this wonderful variety the established principles which regulate human speech, it will be safe to affirm, are the same in all times and in all places the world over. An appeal for approval may be made with confidence to the learned men of Christendom upon this subject, who will be able to judge of the matter in hand by analogy from facts to which attention is to be called. It is not contended that the analogy is perfect, for there is no exact parallel to be found, and the Chinese language is just as different from all other languages as the Chinese people are different from all other peoples. But it is surely not a chimerical expectation, that in the future a common origin may be demonstrated for all peoples and languages on the face of the earth.

It is well known, as has been intimated, that the cultivation and rise of the vulgar tongues in Europe, in religion, science and literature, is comparatively modern; and that there was a long and bitter struggle, indeed hardly yet ended we may say, and a struggle in which the literary classes too were found in great numbers in the ranks of the vanquished, before the mediæval Latin was banished, as to common use, from the churches and schools, as one cause of the ignorance among the common people during the dark ages, and as not adopted to the changed conditions of modern times. Analogous changes it is believed may be expected in China before she can take her proper place among the nations, when what we choose to call the vulgar tongues shall take the place of the present style of literature in favor with the literary classes.

In the discussion of this subject attention must be directed to the distinction between the words Language and Dialect, as often used in this connection. The line which separates them is by no means clearly defined. It will conduce to clearness if the senses intended in this paper are explained, for it is an old question and all the more difficult in view of modern investigations, which show how nearly the different families of human speech and written languages are related in origin and character to each other.

It is not worth while to contend about mere names. The facts are most important. What is meant in this paper by a different Language is such a difference of idiom, pronunciation, &c., as to prevent mutual understanding in conversation or in books where the language has been reduced to writing. By Dialect is meant such a variation as does not prevent a good understanding. It is contended that in this sense there is very much the same state of things to be found in China as in Europe, and it cannot be denied that there is something very like a difference in language to be found in the forms of speech in the Middle Kingdom. For instance; take the specimens referred to in the introduction of Dr. Williams's Syllabic Dictionary — Mandarin, Pekin, Hankow, Shanghai, Ningpo, Fuchau, Amoy, Swatow, and Canton. It may be contended that there is almost, if not fully, as great a difference between at least some of them as there is between the languages of Spain, Portugal, France, and Italy; or say the German, Dutch, and Danish languages, as spoken to-day in Europe. It is believed that the facts when fully known and compared, will warrant the statement that there are many languages as

. well as dialects in China. They have perhaps not yet been sufficiently studied to justify anything like scientific accuracy in statements in regard to their origin, history and character, but certainly it is evident upon a slight knowledge of the subject that there is in many respects a close analogy to be discovered with what is found in other parts of the world. What is called Mandarin, both northern and southern, is spoken, and understood to a great extent over all the northern and central provinces. This vulgar tongue has been reduced to writing and used in books principally in light literature; in novels of different kinds, and in theatrical plays. But one of the finest specimens perhaps is the commentary on the Sacred Edict, and it affords a valid argument in favor of the general import of this paper, that one of the most enlightened emperors of this dynasty chose this style for the work in question, issued by Imperial authority, and ordered to be read at stated periods in every part of the Empire.

Every one of the principal divisions of Chinese speech has a great variety of pronunciation, or as may be represented different dialects. At Canton the natives say, and a foreigner if observing can perceive, that there is a difference between the mode of speech in the western and eastern suburbs. The dialect spoken at Macao differs in one respect from that spoken at Canton, in leaving out the aspirate by the former, as in the case of the dwellers in Gilead and Ephraim on the banks of the Jordan; the one party saying Sibboleth, and the other Shibboleth. But these differences within a large radius of the provincial city are not so great as that of the Yorkshire peasantry from that of their fellows in the south of England. These different modes of speech are not confined to the lower classes, but the same peculiarities belong to the gentry. In this respect it is different from that in Europe.

The classical literature may be said to take the place of the Latin. It is read with different pronunciation in all parts of the

Empire, and may be regarded as not a spoken language, except the most ancient referred to above. The object of this paper is to plead for the cultivation and use of the vulgar tongues, and the preparation of books in the colloquial or vernacular languages. It is believed that the special want of China at present, in order to the elevation of the country to a proud place among the nations, is the cultivation and use in literature of a simple style, something different from that in use now, the reduction to writing of the common speech, of such as in English is called the mother tongue, that which is learned on the mother's breast. What is called the book style is associated with the dismal scenes of the school-room, and the dreadful drudgery of committing to memory page after page, and volume after volume, of sounds without understanding the meaning. The books in the schools are not in the language of common life. The words awaken no sweet memories of home, and there is no music in them to strike the chords of the heart when the sounds are heard by the ear.

1. The first reason for this plea is the connection of this subject with the faithful translation of the Bible, and its use by the people. As an illustration of what may be seen every day in mission work, it may be stated that when the Rev. Mr. Douglas was at Canton doing the work of an evangelist, he called together the native helpers of the different societies in order to address them, of course through an interpreter. As an introduction to the service he requested that a part of a chapter be read from the prophecy of Ezekiel. All who were present would testify that the simple reading of the Chinese version in the book style was quite unintelligible to the greater part of that picked audience, without the book being in their hands. It is surely a reasonable demand that the Bible be translated in a style easy to be understood by the congregation when read from the pulpit. This is not a question of mere taste and preference. We have for our guide the style of the original Hebrew

and Greek, and not only so, but an authorized translation of the Old Testament in the LXX. quoted by the writers of the New Testament. These are inspired models for our imitation, and it may be urged that inspiration has reference to manner as well as to matter. It is safe and a sacred duty for all who believe in the fact of a sacred classic to conform as much as possible to the type of style found in the original. And how simple and lucid and easy to be understood is that style when addressed to the hearing of the ear! How different from the style dear to the heart of the Chinese student of the present day; in reference to the difficulties of which a remark was made by an eminent sinologue, that the Chinese language appeared to be a device of Satan to keep the masses of the people in ignorance, confining knowledge of books to the very narrow circle of a learned class. It is the glory of God, and of the "Word of God," on the other hand, to reveal the highest mysteries to all classes. "The Law and the Prophets" were read in the ears of the people, who were able to understand what they heard. They were instructed, even the children, every Sabbath when they sat in the Synagogue, and heard the reading of the Sacred Rolls.

2.—It is not only important that translations of the Bible be furnished in the vulgar tongues or common speech of the people, but that almost all kinds of literature find representation in this style, even for distribution among the literary classes for their enlightenment in this matter, that not only the truth of Christianity, but all kinds of science and philosophy, may be seen to be within the reach of the multitude, not being dependent upon the mere "wisdom of words" or recommended only by the advantage of a peculiar style. The principles of religion and philosophy, and the facts of modern science may doubtless be taught most effectually by a plain style. Attention must be called to the ideas themselves more than to their expression. There are beauty and majesty in truth itself, and life is more than form. It is an altogether false theory that books and tracts must be cast in the mould of the essay of the Chinese student to recommend the truth of religion and science to the literary classes. It is a poor ambition to show them that Christians may emulate the fine writing of the heathen. Our glory is rather in principles and truth and practical aims. It may be feared, that by the affectation of an elaborate style, the impression may be produced that want of argument and fact is attempted to be concealed under the guise of a fine outward appearance, and it is certain that the Chinese are quite open to conviction as to the real excellence of a plain and simple style. Not long ago a Chinese scholar pointed out to me the impropriety of the style of a new commentary on a part of the Bible, in which he declared the explanations were harder to understand than the text itself.

3.—This subject is intimately connected with the theory and practice of education. According to the principles which are supposed to rule in modern civilization and its best approved systems, those of China to-day are intolerable; but it should be remembered that from the Chinese standpoint, and for the end they have in view, their plan is really the best. As is well known, what is called Education in China has sole reference to success in the literary examinations, without any regard whatever to discipline of mind or attempt to enlarge the boundaries of human knowledge or to communicate it. It consists of training and cramming for the great contest before the Literary Chancellor and Imperial Commissioners, with the one object of obtaining a degree, as a step in the path of official promotion. This is best attained by committing to memory the Classics, commentaries and essays which were considered to be models of excellence at the time. The style of the modern essay affected by the scholars at present is highly unnatural and artificial. It is a perversion of art, strangely grotesque like the Chinese drawings, without perspective, without a touch of nature or genius, and

with altogether too much attention paid to unimportant details. It is a distortion and outrage upon good sense, like the dwarf-trees and plants so offensive to correct taste, in which the really beautiful and graceful bamboo for instance, which grows when left to itself as straight as an arrow, is twisted and bent into most ungainly shapes. All this, in conception and form, is in strict conflict with the spirit and intention of the education demanded by modern civilization. According to the most approved methods, the fullest scope is given to natural dispositions. Nature is fostered and developed. Ideas, thought and truth are to be regarded as above style, as nature is superior to art. The best style is that which is the best vehicle for the clear and rapid communication of thought. Where ideas of truth reign there is the most of beauty and excellence. That is best which is most allied to nature, whose sphere is high and wide as the heavens, for the exhibition of all of nature's wonders; where may be seen the vicissitudes of day and night and the seasons, the storms of passion, with thunder peal and vivid lightning, instead of the confined limits of the student's cell or the examination hall, and the mere dexterity shown in composing that strange product of Chinese study the literary style. Reform is most necessary on this point before the great mass of the people can be taught what is to be known outside of China, or what is to be discovered of the natural resources of their own country. The very nature of the training required for the production of the essay already described is to cramp rather than to aid and develop genius. It is like that curious work of art called mosaic. A recent letter from the Vatican says, " We were shown a very small picture, in which mosaic work was so fine, that the artist had been eight years upon it, and for its completion six years will still be required. Twenty-two thousand shades of color are here used in this art." Perhaps nowhere in the wide world, certainly in no place under the influence of modern civilization, except in this stronghold of the Papacy, could such an art flourish. There is nothing so like it in the world, as the essay of the Chinese literary examinations. The Classics are cut up into all conceivable shapes and worked together, with wonderful skill and patience, like the colored stones in these pictures of mosaic work in the Vatican at Rome. They are very curious, but they are not worthy of a place among treasures of the old masters, nor are they models in any sense fitted to the wants of the present age. They seem out of place within the sound of the locomotive, the power-press of the newspaper and the many other noises in the busy marts of commerce. A little reflection will serve to show that the plea now urged is in behalf of one of the greatest wants of China, for notwithstanding the high estimation in which learning is supposed to be held among the people, it must be remembered, that the whole nation is sunk in ignorance of all true religion and sciences. They have no proper idea of education for its own sake, for the discovery of the truth and for the welfare of the race. They have no idea of the general diffusion of knowledge among the people, the education of women, or indeed of any of those great institutions established in the countries of Christendom for the elevation of the degraded and ignorant classes. They have no provision and no furniture for such work. They have no public assemblies for reading and preaching and teaching. They have no Sabbath or Church services, no lectures, no family worship, no family circle at home, no libraries, and none of those institutions which are the peculiar glory of modern civilization; so they have not felt the need of literature in a plain and simple style. But it is certain the want will be felt when these institutions are introduced; and more than any other thing, the churches, and schools, and families will welcome a translation of the Bible in the language of common life. The action of the Japanese has been wisely commended for their recent resolution

to give up the use of the Chinese character with the design of attaining greater simplicity and cultivating their own language. The use of the vulgar tongues in China in books would possess the same significance. It is a matter for sincere congratulation that the spoken language in the North of China has been reduced to writing, and especially that the Bible has been translated into it. There can be but little doubt that it will quite supersede the translation in the style of the Modern Essay. It has been suggested that this version would answer for the whole Empire, but nothing will suit the requirements of the case except a version in the vulgar tongue, as explained above. It may be stated without fear of contradiction that if the wishes of those who contribute funds for the support of missions in China, and for printing Bibles and tracts were consulted, it would be found that they would vote in an overwhelming majority for a style conformed to the language of common life and such as may be understood when read in the churches, rather than that of the style of the modern essay.

The time cannot be distant when, with all the changes inevitable in the not remote future, the bondage of what is falsely called the Classic style and the mode of education made necessary by it, shall be broken, and books will be prepared teaching the truths of religion and all the sciences in such a language as the children can understand and which may be read in the tones of a mother's voice at the bedside of the dying. With the introduction of Christianity and modern science there will come a great revolution. The new state of things will necessitate a simple style of teaching, and when knowledge is sought for its own sake and for unselfish ends, the scholars will be no more content to spend precious time in committing to memory loads of stupid essays, with the mere intention of improving a style which, when attained, is of questionable value.

In the discussions as to the merit of different translations of the Bible the remark is sometimes heard that some one, more than another, is more pleasing in style to Chinese scholars. Now unless the facts and reasonings of this paper are wide of the mark, such a style instead of being a commendation is just the opposite, for such a style is the worst possible, and to be avoided; and the true model should be, instead of the essay of the student, the colloquial. It may be in some parts of China a mere ideal and not yet reduced to writing, but what is demanded is conformity in some measure at least to the perfection of style as seen in the discourses of Jesus Christ, for the attainment of which, listening to the talk of children is a better preparation than studying the admired models of the present race of Chinese scholars. It is hard to believe that the sacred writers would recognize their own compositions when done up in that style. They appear to better advantage in a simple dress. How admirable the ruddy face and plain garb of the shepherd boy, going with his sling and bag of little stones against the giant Philistine, and how offensive that attention should be diverted from this striking exhibition of faith by the fine workmanship and costly materials of the armor of Saul!

The real working men of science in their investigations, and among themselves, make use of scientific language and algebraic formulas understood only by the initiated, but they have learned the possibility and importance of bringing the results of their investigations to the knowledge of all classes in the simplest forms of speech. Those who know these things can afford to disregard to some extent the prejudices and perverted tastes of the literary classes in China. We cannot yield to them in their dislike of the subject matter of our religion and philosophy, nor should we feel obliged to follow them in their extravagant admiration for a style utterly unfitted to the wants of this age, or listen to any demand that the Bible be given to them only in a form virtu-

ally sealed to the great mass of the people, leaving them dependent upon learned scholars for explanations. We should rather have faith in the cultivation and use of the vulgar tongues and expect the conversion of the students to more practical and sensible methods. They are ignorant of the capabilities of the common speech, of its uses, and how much simplicity is to be preferred in literature to the labored and difficult style in fashion at present. Unless the experience which has resulted in modern civilization is entirely misleading, we may expect a repetition among Eastern nations of what has been seen in the West. By the cultivation and use of the vulgar tongues and simplicity in modes of teaching, great changes may be effected. It is well known how much the English and German languages of to-day are indebted to early translations of the Bible. We may expect the same results for the yet unwritten vulgar tongues of China.

A few objections sometimes urged against the use of Chinese colloquial may be noticed.

1.—The chief objection, to books in the colloquial style, is that they are offensive to the taste of the Chinese literary classes. It is urged that the scholars are the best judges of style, and that it is unwise to go contrary to their feelings in this matter. The fear has been expressed that such a style for the Bible and Christian literature would repel the higher classes and subject the truth to unnecessary contempt. These reflections ought certainly to be regarded; but at the same time it is to be remembered that the Chinese judge only from their own experience, and from their own stand-point. We should be prepared to encounter the opposition, and to answer objections of this character. The native Christians even, and those well disposed to progress and change, may be most sincere in their expressed dislike for this style, because they do not understand all the relations and the real significance of the subject. They should be taught that the reason for such a style is that, in the opinion of those who desire it, the force of the inspired writers may be most faithfully represented in the use of the vulgar tongue rather than by the labored style of the essay. What is wanted is not merely a finely flowing rythm, but a translation of the words, and especially of the particles, in order to express as far as possible the spirit and meaning of the original. And is it not true that the text of the Hebrew and Greek will hardly find adequate expression in any style radically different from that of the Sacred Writers? It is a mistake to suppose that there is no music or beauty in the spoken language when reduced to writing. Who does not know the capability and power of the vulgar tongues that has any acquaintance with the literature of Europe and America? This plea is not made in behalf of anything low or vulgar in the bad sense—not for anything new—not by any means for slang, or for the rogues' language, but for a spoken language reduced to writing, in which there is surely no want of dignity, or compass for the sweetest poetry, the highest eloquence, and the finest writing of every kind within the wide domain of Belles Lettres. Every modern language, that has any literature, owes it to enthusiasm for the common speech. What Dante did for Italy, and Luther and Goethe for Germany, for instance, some one must do for China.

2.—Another form of objection to books in the colloquial style is that it is contrary to the genius of the Chinese mind and involves a change of an altogether radical character. This objection may be met by saying that the change in question is just such as is required by the exigencies of the times. It is really a change to ancient simplicity. It is necessary in order to sympathy with the spirit of modern progress and indispensable as a preparation for the people of China, and its government, to take their proper place in the family of nations. Official papers are comparatively plain and simple, but how clumsy and inappropriate is Chinese letter writing! How utterly destructive of all

true honesty in feeling and sentiment! It is like the dress and ceremonies of their ettiquette. A change is inevitable; and with the disappearance of the long robes and peacocks' feathers in the iron-clads of the navy, and in the ranks of the army, trained in modern drill, will be also the quiet giving up of the present style of composition, so unsuited to the hurry and bustle of this busy age. It may be thought that this article takes an extreme view of the style of writing in fashion at present, and that it shows evidence of a want of appreciation of real excellence. The writer is by no means insensible of certain beauties in the style upon which such severe criticisms are passed. He does not object to it as used by scholars for each other; but he is quite out of patience with the idea that it is the kind of literature for the masses of this Empire. There can be no objection to a version of the Bible in the most concise and labored style of the Essay, if it is meant for a class who can appreciate it, and will read no other: but in his humble opinion it will not be long before such a version would follow the fate of the Vulgate, and be found hardly anywhere, except on the shelves of the student; while versions in the common speech of the people will be found in all the homes of the Empire.

3.—Still another objection is, that an attempt to supply a colloquial literature and versions of the Bible would require an indefinite number. This objection may be met by the statement that, while the dialects may be very numerous, the diversities which are signified in this paper as languages are not very many. All Northern and much of Central China will doubtless use the Mandarin Colloquial. It cannot be used by either the Cantonese or Hakkas, and the statement will probably be verified by facts, to be revealed in the future, that only a few versions will be required for the whole eighteen provinces, and the readers of each may be counted by millions! The time may come before long, when, by modifications, perhaps by the influence of a plain book style conforming to the spoken languages in the newspapers already beginning to multiply as in the West, one style may be used everywhere. But unless the facts and reasonings of this discussion are altogether wide of the mark, that time has not yet come.

4.—Lastly, objections have been urged against Colloquial books because of the imperfections of the attempts which have been made to supply the want in question. But if the object in view be worthy, no one should be deterred by fear of mistakes and blunders, if they lie in the way of ultimate success. It will be an exceedingly difficult work, and doubtless it will be after many failures, before China will be supplied with a version anything like the perfection of the English Bible; but it is believed that it will be reached through the cultivation and use of the vulgar tongues.

In conclusion, it is not strange, in view of all the facts, that pagan scholars, and even that native Christians not yet delivered from the bondage of the past, should protest against the reduction of the spoken language to writing; but it is very strange that any person, acquainted with the history of literature in Europe, should be found to say a word against a corresponding development in China. There can be no doubt in the mind of any one who will study the subject, that the time is not distant, when the literature, now so much praised, in the style of the Essay, will be preserved only as curiosities of a former and bygone age. That which will take its place it is not hard to predict; the decree has gone forth. Without invidious distinctions may it not be said it will be after the model of the English Language. It is the most widely extended, and the most imbued with the Spirit and Genius of Christian civilization. As already intimated this is the eve of the second centennial year of one of the youngest of the family of nations. One of the most significant " signs of the times " is the wonderful diffusion of the spoken and written language of the Anglo Saxon race. The sun never sets upon the dominions of the Beloved Queen, whom all nations delight to honor, and the Republic whose people call Great Britain the " Mother Country," rejoices in the possession of the same literature, and not widely diverse national life. The dwellers on the banks of the Amoor, as they look to the coming dawn, and listen to the voices of the hour, call the *English* speech the *American* language; and so it is, one and the same. They, and all along this coast, the people are watching and waiting for the meeting of the oldest and newest forms of civilization. The Pacific does not separate, but is a high-way. Who will attempt to foretell the result which is to follow this meeting together face to face, of the Lion, the Bear, the Eagle and the Dragon ?

C. F. PRESTON.

TRIP TO THE CITY OF LEEN CHAU.

For a number of years, several of the missionaries of Canton have taken their families into the country, partly for a change after the hot season, to refresh their strength, and partly as a means of exploring the country, and as far as possible to distribute books and tracts and preach to the people in the interior, many of whom never in their lives visit the provincial city. It may interest the readers of the *China Review* if a short account be given of a trip into a region but little known as yet to foreigners. In the present instance the party employed two " Ho Tau " boats. In one were Rev. B. C. Henry and family, Mrs. G. O. Rogers, Miss Galbraith and Johnny Happer; in the other your correspondent and family. Of course on these occasions "the more the merrier." Several families who expected to join the excursion were disappointed, and instead of four or five boats we were reduced to two. We provided our own furniture and food. We had looked forward to it for some time, and abundant preparation was made for an absence of three weeks, more or less according to the weather we should meet.

We started after breakfast on Tuesday, 12th Oct., a little provoked at our inability to impress upon our boatmen at this early stage, the value of time and punctuality. As far as Fatshan we were favored with the company of Rev. Messrs. Selby and Masters, the latter "paddling his own canoe." We made them a call in the new Bungalow of the Wesleyan Mission, and found it an ornament to the suburbs of the city, and well· adapted for the purpose designed, and a great improvement on the native houses used before by the missions at Fatshan. Bidding adieu to these friends we passed through the city, which took a long time, and we were impressed anew with the commercial importance of the city, and in consequence the urgent need for missionary effort there as a centre of influence, we passed into the country beyond. About 4 p.m. a boat coming down with the tide came in collision with one of our boats, carrying away a few timbers and planks from the stern. The trackers ran after the offender for compensation. This claim for damages was quite successful, for although the boatman professed to have no money he yielded up an anchor and line to the satisfaction of the one party and the earnest protest of the other. We spent the night at a place called Wong T'ing. It may be remarked here that we had for our guide copies of a map of the North River made by Rev. J. C. Nevin in 1861, and a sketch of the Leen Chau River made by Rev. H. V. Noyes in June of the present year, when he with his sisters and Miss Crouch made the trip.

Wednesday, 13th.—As the boats in going up stream make but slow progress the boat-

men for the most part track with long lines, all hands have opportunity for long walks on the banks. In the distance begin to loom up the hills of the old coast line, and it is easy to believe that in a not remote past the whole alluvial plain between these hills and the sea was covered by the waves of the ocean and that the land has been reclaimed from the dominion of old Neptune. To the left we see the Sai Chiu Hills, famous for fine scenery and good tea. Near at hand we were able to examine the operations of husbandry. The fields were parched and the crops suffering for want of rain. At one point a crowd came running to ask when they might expect rain. They were evidently much disappointed when told that we could not inform them. They said they thought we must certainly know. At dark we came to anchor off the district city of Sam-Shui 三水, the point at which the North River joins its waters with the West River. This is a very small city, but near by is the large market town of Sai-Nam, which is a very busy place, and the centre of an extensive trade. During the evening a boat came from the Custom-house and accused the boatmen of smuggling salt. The parties who hired the boats had beforehand warned the boatmen that in case any goods were taken they must not expect any help from their passengers but must take all responsibility themselves. The deputies from the Customs station declared, that they understood the case, and that the boatmen must deliver all the salt aboard. After a good deal of loud talking the matter was settled by the giving up of ten bags of salt. These agents of government were well acquainted with some of the party, whom they addressed by name, telling the place of residence and the situation of the chapel in which one is accustomed to preach. They were anxious to know the latest news from Peking and the state of the negociations between the English Minister and the high officials of their own nation.

In talking over the matter afterwards with

the boatmen, they all declared that it was the custom always to take a certain number of bags of salt, no matter who engaged the boats, and that they were seldom molested. Of course we took occasion to remind them of our admonition with a "we told you so," and to warn them "not to do so another time" as it might cause trouble, although we have no objection to their taking a certain amount of cargo if we are in no way responsible for it. If they suppose that smuggling may be carried on under cover of a passport, of course it will not be long before the mistake will be corrected. It would seem that smuggling and corruption were the general rule in this Empire. We heard nothing of any trouble at any of the stations beyond, but it is possible that silver keys unlocked the barriers! We give the information for the benefit of those who come after us. We were certainly in danger of being reckoned smugglers.

Thursday, 14th.—In the morning we commenced the ascent of the North River, leaving the Sai Ch'in Hills in the south, and the fine peak on which the "Ting U" monastery is situated on the left. Our course is parallel with the old coast range, and will continue so until we enter the pass in which the "Fi Loi" monastery is situated. As we pass along the country gradually grows poorer, and it is plain in many ways that we are leaving the rich plains of the lower delta, filled with silk and rice, and entering a region much less fertile and prosperous. A number of brick-kilns are to be seen in this vicinity and further up the river from which Canton is in a measure supplied. Dried grass is used for fuel and many boatloads of unwieldy size were a prominent feature of the landscape. Towards evening we passed Lo Pau 盧包, a place where the tides cease. During high water there is a short cut from this place to Canton. There is an important Customs station here. We spent the night at a little village a short distance above.

Friday, 15th.—To-day the country was very like that seen yesterday, only we were coming nearer the hills. Towards evening we ascended a hill near Shek Kok 石角, some of the party going to the pagoda which may be seen a long distance.

There is a short way to Canton overland from this place and official dispatches are sent by that route. We spent the night almost in the shadow of the hill and pagoda, in a beautiful moonlight. It was then just past the full, and before the moon arose the stars sparkled like gems in the clear pure air.

Saturday, 16th.—In the afternoon we passed the district city of Tsing Un 清遠. The suburbs hide the wall. This place is famous for a kind of brown sugar. We were unable to reach the Fi Loi monastery, and spent the night a little way below the pass.

Sunday, 17th.—In the early morning we came to anchor at the Monastery, where we spent the day and night. It is a most beautiful retreat, perhaps not surpassed by any within the radius of its distance from the provincial city; certainly in many respects this is true. Everything is in miniature, but perfect in its way. After locating the ladies and children in a beautiful spot at the foot of a water-fall, under the shade of fine old forest trees, the two missionaries of the party started off in quest of people to carry to them the "good tidings" of Christianity. At the entrance of the pass is a small village. We first gave a tract to each shop and notice that an address would be given at one of the temples. It was noticed with much pain that connected with almost all the shops were dens for opium-smoking or gambling, and as might be expected under such conditions evidences on every side of great poverty, and with no signs of thrift or comfort. We succeeded in gathering a goodly number of people and an attentive audience. It was natural under the circumstances to give emphasis to the facts which had so painfully impressed us, and in our discourse we endeavoured to point out the connection which exists between true religion and good morals—and that with the spread of Christianity might be expected a change in the customs of the people—instead of these dens for opium-smoking and gambling, there would be happy homes and improved social life in every way. After a long service some time was spent in answering questions and free conversation, we returned to the Monastery—there we conversed with the priests, and had a service with the boatmen who clamored for it for themselves. Allusion was made to the subject which had gained attention in the morning. We tried to urge upon the priests to take a stand upon the opium question, to forbid its use in the monastery and then to carry the reform into the region about. It is to be feared that at least for the present little practical result will follow. But the time is not distant when the Chinese of all classes will be compelled to give earnest heed to the subject.

Monday, 18th.—In the early morning three of the party made an ascent of the highest peak in the rear of the Monastery, taking the barometer with them; at the water line it stood at 30°, and at the highest point 28°—a fall of two inches, making about 1,850 feet elevation. We left at 9 a.m. The scenery at this point is very fine indeed. We spent the night just below the Censer Pass.

Tuesday, 19th.—The scenery in the Censer Pass is more tame than that at Fi Loi—or that beyond called the "Blind Boy Pass." The mouth of the Leen-chau River is at the entrance of this last. We spent the night at this point. Our attention was called to a quarry of the fine granite so much thought of at Canton, called "Leen-chau blue stone." We found a man who had just purchased a hand rice-mill to take to his home at the Mei Ling Pass. He said it could be used in a family for several generations without wearing out! The workmen were very friendly, asking and answering questions as long as we had time to stop with them.

Wednesday, 20th.—In the morning two small boats joined our party engaged by the boatmen, to which they transferred their cargo of smuggled salt. The rapids on this river are very numerous and shallow, allowing nothing but very light draft. We were this day first made acquainted with the rapids of the river. Indeed the river may be said almost to be a succession of rapids—some of them with a very swift current. The water is clear as crystal, and the bed is composed of boulders. During the afternoon the party had a long walk through the fields. The country people were many of them much frightened. We were especially interested in one woman who clung to the hand of her brother, as if her very life were at stake. Among other things we found the cotton plant—some in flower and some in perfection. Near at hand were lime-kilns, fields of sugar-cane, peanuts and buckwheat. Instead of rice we saw large patches of Indian corn. From all accounts what is raised is altogether insufficient for home consumption. When attempting to make purchases we were told that if they sold their produce they would not have sufficient for themselves. Parties intending to make the trip are to be advised to make provision without reference to obtaining anything on the way. We were astonished to find difficulty in obtaining even chickens and eggs. Near the place where we spent the night, a rock—a fine stalactite—was pointed out to us called "Priest with head hanging downwards."

Thursday, 21st.—The scenery is continually changing. The hills are full of holes and caves and clefts and rugged rocks. Near evening we passed a place called Ham Kwong 合光 an important custom station, with a bridge of boats, like one at Shiu Kwan on the North River. This barrier is opened generally only once a day, except for officials. It was opened for us after producing our passport and requesting the favor. It is evidently a place of some importance. We found it very noisy—chiefly it was said on account of a theatre at the time in operation. We spent the night in the vicinity, and the next day we met with many people going to town to attend the theatrical performance.

Friday, 22nd.—To-day the boats were delayed a long time passing one rapid. Some of the party had long walks on the banks and conversations with the people—especially with a crowd near the market town of Sam Kong 三江, where the story of the Prodigal Son was told, with evident interest to the hearers. Once in a while a person was met who had been to Canton and heard of Christian teaching, but the great mass have never been much beyond 'the boundary of their local horizon, and preaching was quite a new thing. We saw during the day many large wheels propelled by the current used for elevating water into the fields, rude machinery, but a much better method than man or even bullock power working the chain-pump. Where the current is not swift enough to serve the purpose a good steam pump would be a real saving, and the outlay would doubtless be a real economy, besides relieving human beings in a measure from unnecessary toil. Christian civilization aims to change mere beasts of burden into men, who are the image of their Maker. Oh what a change will be wrought when these regions are filled with Christian institutions, the home, the school and the Church! How much poverty and vice and misery now. How much wealth and goodness and happiness there might be. We passed the night near Ma Po Hü 麻布墟 or the "Linen cloth market."

Saturday, 23rd.—No special incident this day, only infinite variety in hill, and rock, and rapid, and pass. We came to anchor near a small hamlet at the foot of high hills.

Sunday, 24th.—Here we spent a quiet Sabbath. Not far from the boats under shady trees was found a pretty nook, with the perpetual music of a water-fall, and concealed by a low hill was a glen of marvelous beauty, which the ladies wished to name Sabbath Glen. These little glimpses

of fine scenery convinced the party that many places, which appear in passing only barren mountain, if explored, would be found to be very gems of beauty. Books were distributed to the people of the hamlet, and a service held in their poor apology for a school house. The teacher was a young man who appeared open to conviction and willing to listen to religious conversation. Another service was held with the boatmen in the afternoon.

Monday, 25th.—To-day the scenery was particularly fine, and full of interest. The hills on both sides were higher and more rugged. One high hill of rock standing on the bank is called by the Chinese "The Fisherman" 釣魚工. On one of the hills in this vicinity is a silver mine, which was pointed out to us, the mouth closed with masonry, and sealed with the seals of the officials, all safe for a future time when it will be possible to work it with profit. The boatmen said that when it was worked the cost of the ore was about equal to the amount of precious metal obtained. It is quite probable that superstition had something to do with shutting it up. There is an immense treasure of coal and other valuable treasure in this empire awaiting the coming of a Christian civilization before it can be unlocked. On another hill was a fortified eminence, or high place. The people said it had been a Robber's Den, but it may have been a place of refuge from robbers. The mountains here are full of caves and dens, that might be so used, and it is plain that many of them, within recent times too, have been used as means of defence against rebels and robbers. Crossing the river opposite to this fortified rock we visited an open cave of considerable size. The same day we passed two important market towns, and came to anchor not far above a remarkably-shaped hill of rock, which we found marked on our sketch as the Giant's Thumb. The Chinese call it the "Genii General." Our party, taking another peak close at hand, chose to call them monk and nun, shrouded with mantle and hood. In some places here the echoes were very fine, and the children, to say nothing of the elder members of the party, found much amusement in the reflection of loud shouts and screaming. In the dusk of the evening several of the enterprising spirits took a climb on a hillside. Coming suddenly upon some Chinese women they created great terror, so as to cause one of her protectors of the sterner sex to shoulder a big club to resist the invaders. A few kind words served to allay the agitation and to call forth a request for medical treatment. The fame of the missionary hospitals has spread far into the interior. During the evening an elder from one of the villages made us a visit, bringing some of his friends. We had an exceedingly interesting and satisfactory interview, in which many questions were asked and answered. He said business called him once in two or three years to Canton, and the next time he made the visit, he should be sure to find us out. His ancestors were from the Fukien province.

Tuesday, 26th.—Another long walk today. Large fields of peanuts and Indian corn, with now and then a patch of sugar cane, were seen at the foot of the hills. There were also many of the large water-wheels pumping the crystal stream into the parched fields. We anchored a little while at the district city of Yeung Shan 陽 山, a very small place indeed, but with a rather imposing looking wall in fine repair. We distributed books and were urged to spend the day and preach. We determined to stop on our return if possible, to have a talk with them. We spent the night within sight of what is put down on our sketch as the "Cathedral Cave," called by the Chinese the Ngau Ngam or "Ox Cave." I should have mentioned two peaks seen from the district city of Yeung Shan, called by our friends who came before us the Siamese Twins, which we all thought a very good name. During the evening our attention was called to boats

fishing with cormorants. At night bright torches are used. We were told that fish caught by them had an unpleasant odor communicated to them by the bird. We saw many fishing with nets, and in some cases driving the fish into them by making rattling noises. I saw one man with a long line and reel, which looked like home. I wondered if this implement of western anglers, like many other inventions, could be claimed as an invention of the Chinese. It was a rough enough apology for such as are used by professional people in England and the United States, but it evidently served the purpose desired well enough. I was sorry not to be able to see how the thing worked.

Wednesday 27th.—In the early morning before breakfast we climbed up the hillside to explore the grand cave for ourselves, and I may as well say beforehand that we were not disappointed. The glowing accounts we had heard we felt were fully justified by the splendid sights to be seen. We found it a hard climb to get to the mouth, but as soon as we looked in all exclaimed that the labor of the ascent was not in vain. It is to regretted that we made no measurements, but we will leave the scientific description to others who will follow. Suffice it to say that the entrance is like a grand hall, with immense pillars, perhaps 75 feet in height, and 8 or 10 feet in diameter. All the furniture of the most elaborately finished cathedral might with the aid of a little imagination be found here. The Chinese call it also the Cave of the Genii, and what is not at all unlike a shrine is pointed out as the seat of the idol. Perhaps the finest part is exposed to the light of the sun, but there are many very pretty rooms and niches found by exploring within with torches, and some points where the echoes are very fine indeed. The formations of stalactites and stalagmites in this cave are wonderful. Some like immense folds of drapery, and then you can imagine lamps, and thrones, and windows of all shapes and sizes. We left with regret, and look back upon this as the finest part of the excursion. It is strange that the Chinese have left this wonder in its natural state. There is no Chinese art to disfigure nature here, and there is not even a path made to lead to it. The remainder of the day was spent laboring against the swift current of the rapids. We spent the night not far below the Hot Springs.

Thursday, 28th.—In the morning we came to the Hot Springs, holes in the rock just above the level of the stream as it then was. Of course during high water these would be covered. Up on the bank only a little removed from the river was a larger spring, perhaps six or eight feet in diameter. At this season the water was only luke-warm, perhaps a little above blood heat, certainly not like the spring near Macao in which some years ago I boiled some eggs. The people in the vicinity said that during cold weather the temperature was much higher. It is quite possible that was true only in appearance. One of the boatmen remarked in all simplicity that the people of that village were indeed well favored, since, when they gave their daughters in marriage, it was unnecessary to use fuel to heat water for their bath! Several practical minds suggested that there was a good place for washing clothes. We could discover no medical properties by the taste. Some of the boatmen gave evidence of thought by inquiring the cause of the phenomenon, which was a pleasant variation from the gross and unappreciative suggestions mentioned above. We had not gone far before we came to what is called the Dragon Cave, said to be the greatest curiosity in all this region. I have little doubt of the fact, but our party had neither the time nor disposition to verify the claim. An inscription declares that it extends sixty *li* or twenty miles. Some of the party explored it with torches a few hundred feet, and reported a large chamber fully as large as that of the Cathedral Cave. A number of workmen were engaged repairing the temple at the

entrance. There is good landing and stone steps leading to the mouth. It would be worth while to have a thorough exploration of this extensive cavern in the bowels of the earth. On the same day we visited the "*Kun Yam*" Cave, chiefly interesting to the Chinese from its idolatrous associations. We explored it for a short distance with torches but with no particular satisfaction. Indeed the fire of enthusiasm does not burn very brightly after being in these dark places for a little while; like the torches it pales for a time and is then extinguished. The night was spent at the lower end of the Yeung Tiu Hap 羊跳峽, so called from its being so narrow in one place that a goat might jump across.

Friday, 29th.—We found this pass in the morning really very fine indeed, full of strange and beautiful views. There were several tiny water-falls, coming down in broken spray like bridal veils. It was wonderful to see the varieties of ferns and wild flowers. Among others we noticed the Oleander. Altogether it was quite weird, fairy-like, and different from anything we had seen before. These hills ought to be covered with flocks of sheep and goats. It is said they once were, and there can be little doubt that in the future in better times they will rejoice with plenty instead of lying waste as at present. Not far beyond is the last pass of our trip. It is called the "Ma Miu Hap" 馬廟峽. It is very like the last described and is named from a niche in the face of one of the hills of rock within which, as the boatmen pointed out, could be seen a striking likeness of a horse and rider fully equipped; with but little aid of the imagination this may be seen as if it were a piece of statuary by one of the old masters. It gives the name to the beautiful pass in which it is found, "Pass of the temple to the horse." As we emerged from this narrow gorge we soon caught a glimpse of the pagoda on a hill overlooking the city of Leen Chau, the end of our journey.

Ascending slowly the last rapid we came to the foot of the hill on which is the pagoda. Most of the party climbed the hill, from which a most magnificent view was obtained of the surrounding country. The city lay almost at our feet, wide fields cultivated like gardens are seen near at hand, dotted here and there by village and hamlet. From this height and at distance they looked trim and clean. We knew that they were filled with squalor and dirt, and that it was distance which lent enchantment to the view. Beyond and stretching far away we could see the hills and ranges of blue mountains which constitute the northern boundary of the Canton province, in which are many tribes of the Miutsz or aborigines. They are often seen in Leen Chau.

Here it was plain enough to find what our friends had called the "Old man of the mountains." His mammoth profile was drawn on one of the mountains to the right, and is not a poor representation, but not equal to the famous namesake in the White Mountains in the United States. In the afternoon the whole party, except one of the children and the baby, determined to visit the city, taking a supply of books and tracts. After a pleasant walk through the open fields, seeing orange trees full of golden fruit and peach trees in blossom, we came to the suburbs of the city. So far as we know it was the first time foreign ladies and children had appeared in this place. It was not strange that before passing many streets we found ourselves in the midst of a great crowd of people,—too great for comfort or indeed for moving at all. There was nothing left in such a case but to retrace our steps and retire from the increasing multitude. On the part of the ladies and children the retreat was made in good order, the two missionaries covering the retreat by remaining to finish the distribution of books and tracts. When we rejoined our forces the gentlemen found the ladies engaged in conversation with the Chinese women on a grassy knoll by the side of one of the fields near the suburbs. The excursion was thus a success even to the very end. We found the people exceedingly pleasant and respectful, and what is a very important consideration and a happy discovery to us all, it was found that the dialect spoken at the provincial city was well understood everywhere. In some of the villages there were variations, but all understood and praised the speech of the capital of the province. This fact may be explained perhaps by the large emigration from Canton to all the places on the river where there is any trade, and of course the emigrants carry their speech with them.

Saturday, 30th.—All hearts were now turned homewards, perhaps 300 miles away—only the purchase of a few supplies, chickens, quails, eggs, &c., kept us until 10 a.m., when with a favorable wind we started down stream. All was now familiar; we could not walk fast enough to keep up with the boats, but it was pleasant indeed to sit on the top of them and study the varying aspects of the scenery.

Sunday, 31st.—In the morning we ran down to the Small River market town 小江. It was market day, and great crowds of people were found. Books were distributed and a service held in front of a temple in the place. In the afternoon we proceeded on our way as far as the district city of Yang Shan 陽山 where we had been urged to preach. Directly upon landing we were escorted to the Office of the District Magistrate, in front of which we were requested to hold forth. A goodly number of people assembled who listened respectfully as long as strength and voice held out with the speaker. The usual questions at both services were asked in regard to the Opium and Coolie Trade, and answered to the apparent satisfaction of all present. There is also a strong impression on the minds of the masses that the real object of going into the interior is to search for some kind of hid treasure or some precious thing, or to spy out the "Fung-shui" of the country. In fact, a kind of undefined dread of some sinister design has possession of the people, and it will not be removed without a better acquaintance with the outside world, and of the Christian system.

Monday, Nov. 1st.—With the north wind blowing fresh and the strong current in our favor we made a good run. At some of the rapids we were obliged to wait for boats coming up which blocked the channel. Of course the boats coming up have the right of way, and on this account we were several times delayed. We spent the night at Ham Kwong.

Tuesday, 2nd.—We were delayed for a little time in the morning waiting for the barrier at the Custom Station to be opened, but before night we found ourselves a little below the Blind Boy's Pass in the North River, where we spent the night.

Wednesday, 3rd.—About noon we arrived at Fi Loi monastery, where we stopped for a few moments to pay our respects to the priests and to renew our admonitions in regard to Opium smoking and active benevolence. It was already dark before we came to anchor among the boats at Shek Kok.

In the shadows of the coming night one of the Captains spun yarns about river pirates, snake boats &c. For several years the country has suffered much less than formerly from these pests of Chinese society, and we had little cause for fear.

Thursday, 4th.—We reached the West River about noon, and were obliged to change our course and keep along by tracking with the long line again. We spent the night at Tsz Tung, an important place which gives its name to a class of boats at Canton used for picnics, and excursions into the country.

Friday, 5th.—Passing through Fatshan in the forenoon we continued tracking and poling all the way to Canton, where we arrived about 4 p.m. We had been absent nearly a month, and had all the news of the world to pick up as best we could, for no news had reached us during our trip.

The pleasure experienced may be imagined from the expressed desire of all to go again next year to explore in some other direction, when we hope to have a larger company, and no smuggling!

C. F. PRESTON.

LEGEND OF THE BUILDING OF PEKING;

OR,

THE PURSUIT OF THE WATER.

When the Yüan 元, dynasty was destroyed, and Hung-wu 洪 武,' had succeeded in firmly establishing that of the Great Ming 大 明, he made Chin-ling† his capital, and held his court there with great splendour; envoys from all nations, and officers from every province within the "four seas"† assembling there to witness

* 金陵; the present Nanking.

† 四海; China, the empire; everywhere.

his greatness and to prostrate themselves before the "Dragon Throne."*

The Emperor had many sons and daughters by his different consorts and concubines; each mother, in her inmost heart, fondly hoping that her son would be the fortunate prince selected by his father to fill the lofty position occupied by him, when death should call him to a more lofty place—in heaven.

* 龍位; the imperial throne is styled thus.

Although the Empress had a son, who would in the common course of events doubtless succeed to the throne, yet she felt envious of those ladies who had likewise been blessed with children, for fear one of the princes should supplant her son in the affection of the emperor and in the succession. This envy displayed itself on every occasion that offered; she was greatly beloved by the Emperor, and she exerted all her influence with him, as the other young princes grew up, to get them removed from court. Through her means, most of them were sent to the different provinces, as governors; these provinces, under their government, were considered as so many principalities or kingdoms.

One of the consorts of *Hung-wu*, the Lady *Wêng*, 翁, had a son, named *Chu-li* 朱棣. This young prince was very handsome and graceful in his deportment; and was, moreover, of an amiable disposition. He was the fourth son of the Emperor, and his pleasing manner and address had made him a great favourite, not only with his father, but with every one about the court. The Empress noted the evident affection the emperor evinced for this prince, and determined to get him removed from the court as soon as possible. By a judicious use of flattery and cajolery, she ultimately persuaded the Emperor to appoint the prince governor of the Yen, 燕, country, and from henceforth he was styled the prince of Yen.*

It is of this prince that I shall speak only; he is the hero of the tale.

The young prince, shortly after, taking an affectionate leave of the Emperor, left Chinling to proceed to his post. Ere he departed, however, a Taoist priest, named *Liu-po-wên* 劉伯溫, who had a great affection for the prince, put a sealed packet into his hand, and told him to open it when he found himself in difficulty, distress, or danger, and the perusal of the first portion that came to

his hand would invariably suggest some remedy for the evil, whatever it was. After doing so, he was again to seal the packet up, without looking further into its contents, till some other emergency arose necessitating advice or assistance, when he would again find it.* The prince, thanking the old priest for his kindness, departed on his journey, and in the course of time, without meeting any adventures worth recording, he safely arrived at his destination.

The place where Peking now stands was originally called Yu-chou, 幽州; in the T'ang dynasty it was called Pei-p'ing-fu, 北平府; it afterwards became known as Shun-t'ien-fu, 順天府—but this was after the city now called Peking was built. The name of the country in which this place was situated was Yen, 燕. It was a mere barren wilderness, with very few inhabitants; these lived in huts and scattered hamlets, but there was no city to afford protection to the people and to check the depredations of robbers.

When the prince saw what a desolate looking place he had been appointed to, and thought of the long years he was probably destined to spend there, he grew very melancholy, and nothing his attendants essayed to do in hopes of alleviating it succeeded.

All at once the prince bethought himself of the packet which the old Taoist priest had given him; he at once proceeded to make search for it—for in the bustle and excitement of travelling he had forgotten all about it, till his discontent and dislike of the place he had been sent to brought it to his memory, in hopes it might suggest something to better the prospects before him. Having found the packet he hastily broke it open to see what instructions it contained; taking out the first paper which came to hand, he read the following:—

"When you reach Pei-p'ing-fu you must build a city there and name it No-cha

---

* 燕王; the name he is generally known by in the earlier portion of his career.

* In some books it states that *Liu-po-wên* accompanied the prince, and assisted him by his advice.

Chêng,' 哪吒城, (the city of No-cha). But, as the work will cost a great deal of money, you must issue a proclamation inviting the wealthy to subscribe the necessary funds for building it. At the back of this paper is a plan of the city; you must be careful to act according to the instructions accompanying it."

The prince inspected the plan, carefully read the instructions, and found even the minutest details fully explained. He was struck with the grandeur of the design of the proposed city, and at once acted on the instructions contained in the packet; proclamations were posted up, and large sums were speedily subscribed; ten† of the most wealthy families who had accompanied him from Chinling being the largest contributors, supporting the plan not only with their purses, by giving immense sums, but by their influence among their less wealthy neighbours.

When sufficient money was subscribed, a propitious day was chosen on which to commence the undertaking. Trenches, where the foundations of the walls were to be,

were first dug out, according to the plan found in the packet. The foundations themselves consisted of layers of stone, quarried from the Western Hills; bricks of an immense size were made and burnt in the neighbourhood; the moat was dug out, and the earth from thence used to fill in the centre of the walls, which, when complete, were forty *li* in circumference, fifty cubits in height and fifty in breadth; the whole circuit of the walls having battlements and embrasures. Above each of the nine gates of the city immense three-storied towers were built, each tower being 99 cubits in height.†

Near the front entrance of the city, facing each other, were built the temples of Heaven and of Earth. In rear of it was the beautiful "Coal Hill"‡ raised; while in the square in front of the Great Gate of the palace was buried an immense quantity of charcoal.§

The palace was built in a style of exceeding splendour, containing many superb

* No-cha was a third son of *Li-ching*, 李靖, a warrior of the Chou dynasty, some 1200 years B.C. He was born a "ball of flesh;" on his father cutting this ball, it assumed the human form and was endowed with extraordinary powers, for the young No-cha could at once walk or talk and perform various feats. This prodigy died when only seven years of age. Some say that his father killed him, others that he died by his own hand; that he "cut off his flesh to restore it to his mother, and dissevered his bones to return them to his father." He was afterwards made a deity. Sometimes he is represented as having three heads and six or eight arms; oftener, as the accompanying sketch shews, a good-looking child, one hand grasping a fiery brand, and his feet resting on two "fiery wheels." on which he is supposed to ride through the skies. He is the God of Braid Manufacturers, and was the first inventor of Sashes, having made one for his father by braiding the sinews of dragons which he had slain when he was only five days old. The two characters representing his name are written in various manners; in this place those in the Chinese original are used.

† The names of these are given in the Chinese version; among them is found that of the celebrated Nanking Crœsus, *Shên-wan-san*, 沈 萬 三.

* The Chinese version states only 40 *li*—the city is 48 *li* in circumference.

† With the exception of Pagodas, no building is allowed to reach up to 100 cubits in height (anything below that is allowed). This would not only be setting at nought all rules of *féng-shui*, but to do so would be considered as trespassing on heaven's domain, or, as the Chinese say 進天火氣, "entering heaven's caloric" (fire-air or atmosphere.)

‡ Better known as "Prospect Hill." The coal was brought from the Western Hills, piled up, and afterwards covered with earth, planted with trees, and pavilions &c. built on it. The steps leading to the top of the hill are made of large blocks of coal. At the foot of the hill, which is three li round, there is a large hall named Shou-'huang-tien, 壽 皇 殿, (Longevity-imperial-hall) in which an emperor or empress, when they die, are laid out in state.

§ This square or enclosure is surrounded by stone palisades, and is known by the name of Ch'i-p'an-chieh, 棋 盤 街, (Chess-board-street). The bed of charcoal which is buried there is commonly call the T'an-'hai, 炭 海, (Charcoal-Sea). Chinese say that charcoal will never decay, no matter how long it may have been buried. It is probable that the coal and charcoal may have been stored up in this manner in case of such a contingency as the city being besieged for any length of time.

buildings; in the various enclosures were beautiful gardens and lakes; in the different courtyards, too, were 72' wells dug and 36† golden tanks placed. The whole of the buildings and grounds were surrounded by a lofty wall, and a stone-paved moat, in which the lotus and other flowers bloomed in great beauty and profusion, and in the clear waters of which myriads of gold and silver fish disported themselves.

The geomancy of the city was similar to that of Chin-ling. When everything was completed the prince compared it with the plan and found the city tallied with it in every respect. He was much delighted, and called for the ten wealthy persons who had been the chief contributors, and gave each of them a pair of "couchant dragon cuffs,"‡ and allowed them great privileges. Up to the present time there is the common saying "Since then the 'dragon cuffed' gentlefolks have flourished."

The next day the prince returned thanks to the local god; the nine gates of the city were hung with banners and tablets. All the people were loud in praise of the beauty and strength of the newly-built city. The 72§ trades peacefully and profitably went on

with their various avocations. Merchants from every province hastened to Peking, attracted by the news they heard of its magnificence, and the prospect there was of profitably disposing of their wares. In short, the people were prosperous and happy, food was plentiful, the troops brave, the monarch just, his ministers virtuous, and all enjoyed the blessings of peace.

While everything was thus tranquil, and the work all completed, a sudden and untoward event occurred which spread dismay and consternation on all sides. One day, when the prince went into the hall of audience, one of his ministers reported that "the wells were thirsty and the rivers dried up"—there was no water, and the people were all in the greatest alarm. The prince at once called his counsellors together to devise some means of remedying this calamity and cause the water to return to the wells and springs, but no one could suggest a plan for replenishing them.

It is necessary to explain the cause of this scarcity of water. There was a dragon's cave outside the Eastern Wicket* of the city at a place named Lei-chên-k'ou.† The dragon had not been seen for myriads of years, yet it was well known that he lived there.

In digging the earth out to build the wall the workmen had broken into this dragon's cave, little thinking of the consequences which would result from the circumstance. The dragon was exceedingly wroth and determined to shift his abode, but the "she dragon" said, "We have lived here thousands of years, and shall we suffer the prince of Yen to drive us forth thus? If we do go from hence we will take the water with us. Let us cause the river to dry up, the wells to become empty, and let us leave Peking without a drop of water in the whole place; so that, if our privacy is broken in upon and

---

* These are supposed to represent malignant stars; they were formerly spirits which had been shut up in a well, and were released during the Sung dynasty. These 108 all became rebel chiefs. See 水滸傳.

† My informant has seen some of these golden tanks, and relates the following anecdote:— "One of the imperial chair-bearers was caught in the act of scraping the gold off one of the tanks with a knife. On being questioned concerning it, he pleaded in excuse that his wife wanted a hair-pin, and as he was too poor to gratify her by purchasing it, he had resorted to this method to procure the necessary funds. On account of his long service, instead of suffering death, the man was merely expelled the palace. This was in Tao-kuang's reign; my informant not only remembers the circumstance, but also knew the man. At the present time the tanks do service as "dust-bins," any filth and garbage being thrown into them. Originally they were intended to contain a supply of water, as a precaution, in case of fire.

‡ 壹副團龍袖, Silk or satin cuffs, with the dragon embroidered on them.

§ Trades or professions of every sort.

* 東便門.

† 雷震口, "Thunder-clap-mouth," name of a small village.

we cannot live here ourselves, the prince and his people, also, shall not be able to do so. We will collect all the water, place it in our 'Yin yang baskets,'* and at midnight we will appear in a dream to the prince, requesting permission to retire. If he gives us permission to do so, and allows us also to take our baskets of water with us, he will fall into our trap, for we shall take the water with his own consent."

The two dragons then transformed themselves into an old man and an old woman, went to the chamber of the prince, who was asleep, and appeared to him in a dream. Kneeling before him they cried, "Thousand Years, Ten Thousand Years,† we have come before you to beg leave to retire from this place, and to beseech you out of your great bounty to give us permission to take these two baskets of water with us."

The prince gave them the required permission at once, little dreaming of the danger he was incurring. The dragons were highly delighted, and hastened out of the presence; filled the baskets with all the water there was in Peking, and carried them off with them.

When the prince awoke from this dream, he thought it very strange, but paid no more attention to it, till he heard the report of the scarcity of water, when, reflecting on the singularity of his dream, he thought there might be some hidden meaning in it, in connection with the deficiency of water, with which he was unacquainted. He, therefore, had recourse to the packet again, and discovered by it that his dream visitors had been dragons, who had taken the waters of Peking away with them in their magic baskets; the packet, however, contained directions what to do to recover the water, and he at once obeyed these directions.

* 陰陽, Male and female principle of nature. Baskets are used in the north to draw water, also to carry oil and other liquids.

† 千歲, a title of kings and princes. 萬歲, the emperor. These are in common use.

In haste the prince donned his armour, mounted his black steed, and spear in hand dashed out of the city gate* in pursuit of the water. He pressed on his horse, which went swift as the wind, nor did he slacken speed till he came up with the water-stealing dragons, who still retained the forms they had appeared to him in his dream. On a cart were also the two identical baskets he had seen; in front of the cart, dragging it, was the old woman, while behind, pushing it, was the old man.

When the prince saw them, he galloped up to the cart, and without pausing, thrust his spear into one of the baskets, making a great hole in it, out of which the water rushed so rapidly that the prince was much frightened, and dashed off at full speed, to save himself from being swallowed up by the waters, which in a very short time had risen more than 30 feet in height and flooded the surrounding country. On galloped the prince, followed by the roaring water till he reached a hill up which he pressed his startled horse. When he gained the top of the hill, he found that it stood out of the water like an island, for the water had completely surrounded it, and was seething and whirling round the hill in a frightful manner, but no vestige could he see of either of the dragons.

The prince was very much alarmed at his perilous position, when, suddenly, a Buddhist priest appeared before him, with clasped hands and bent head, who bade him not be alarmed, as with Heaven's assistance he would soon disperse the water. Hereupon, the priest recited a short prayer or spell and the waters receded as rapidly as they had risen, and finally returned to their proper channels.

The broken basket became a large deep hole, of some three Mu† in extent, in the centre of which was a fountain which threw

* Out of the 西直門, (Western Straight Gate).

† About half-an-English acre. One mu being about the sixth of an acre.

up a vast body of clear water. From the midst of this there arose a pagoda, which rose and fell with the water, floating on the top like a vessel; the spire thrusting itself far up into the sky, and swaying about like the mast of a ship in a storm.

The prince returned to the city filled with wonder at what he had seen, and joy at having so successfully carried out the directions contained in the packet. On all sides he was greeted by the acclamations of the people, who hailed him as the saviour of Peking. Since that time Peking has never had the misfortune to be without water.

The Pagoda is called the "Imperial Spring Mountain Pagoda." The spring is still

* 卸 泉 山 塔; more commonly called Chên-shui-ta, 鎮水塔. This pagoda is dis-

there, and day and night, unceasingly, its clear waters bubble up and flow eastwards to Peking, which would now be a barren wilderness, but for "Yen-wang's pursuit of the water."*

G. C. STENT.

tant about twenty li from Peking. It is on the top of the hill, while the spring is at the foot half a li distant. The imperial family use the water from this spring, from whence it is carried to Peking in carts.

* Others say that Kao-liang 高亮, a soldier of low rank at that time, is the hero of the "pursuit of the water," but that he was drowned after spearing the water basket. He had successfully performed his task, and was galloping back to Peking, when, like Lot's wife, he "looked behind him" (having been prohibited from doing so), and the waters at once overwhelmed him. His tomb may be seen to this day; it is half way between the "Western Straight Gate" and the "Great Bell Temple." A bridge near the Hsi-chih-mên is also named Kao-liang's Bridge, in commemoration of his death.

CHINESE EXPLORATIONS OF THE INDIAN OCEAN DURING THE FIFTEENTH CENTURY.

(Continued from page 67.)

IV.

III. Kwa-wa 瓜哇 (Java*).—According to the Geographical Memoirs of the Ming dynasty, this is the same as the

* The intelligent Chinese scholars employed in the administration of this splendid colonial possession of Holland have not been indifferent to the sources of information relating to the early history of the island which Chinese literature affords, and Dr. Gustav Schlegel, in particular, has devoted much attention to this subject. In a small *brochure* published at Batavia in 1870, under the title "*Jets omtrent de Betrekkingen der Chinezen met Java, voor de Komst der Europeanen aldaar*," Dr. Schlegel has presented the Chinese text, accompanied by a version in Dutch from his own pen, of a description of Java compiled at Peking on his behalf from existing records. The Chronicle of the Ming dynasty was in all probability consulted for the materials thus obtained, but the original authorities were no other than those from which the text now followed was compiled, as is evident from the

country anciently known as Shê-p'o.' The chapter on Java in the Chronicle of the Yüan dynasty states that one who embarks at Ts'üan-chow† proceeds first to Chan-eh'êng (Champa) and thence on to this country.

This country lies south of Champa it may be one thousand li.‡ Sailing from Champa the course is steered for Ling-shan,§ where

fact that the particulars narrated and the language used are in both cases almost absolutely the same.

* 闍 婆 read Shê-wa. See Note I. at foot.
† 泉 州 See Note II. at foot.
‡ So in the text. The character for "one" is perhaps a misprint for "seven," which would be more nearly correct.
§ See note to Part II., 322. Since this note was published, however, the writer has seen reason to identify the headland of Ling-shan with

the depth of water is about sixty fathoms.
In fifty watches more, Wu-kung Yü ("Cen-
tipede" Island) is reached; and five watches
westward from the rocks at the point of this
island bring the vessel to Mao-shan. Again
ten watches, and the eastern Shé-lung-shan
("Serpent and Dragon" Headland) is sight-
ed, after which the vessel passes between
Round Island and Double Island. Passing
by Lo-wei-shan, where there are eighteen
fathoms of water, five watches more bring
the vessel to "Bamboo" Island, and thence,
in five watches, Ki-lung Yü* ("Hen-coop"
Island) is reached. From this point it is ten
watches to Kow-lan-shan,† where wood and

Cape Varela, lat. 12.° 55′, long 109.° 30′ E.,
described by Crawfurd as "the most remarkable
point of Cochin Chinese navigation." (*Embassy
to Siam and Cochin China*, I., p. 352). Charts,
both Chinese and English, which have come into
the writer's possession since the publication of
Part II., leave no farther doubt respecting the
identity of Wai-lo-shan, therein mentioned, with
Cape Touron, and Sin-chow-kiang, therefore,
with Touron Harbour. The Ku-lao rock 古老
石, mentioned in the same note, is Cham Collao,
in lat. 16° N., close to which a small island is
marked on our Admiralty charts as Goat Island
—probably the 羊 嶼 of the Chinese text.

* The distinction drawn in the text between
山, which may signify either a large island, a
headland, or simply a mountain, and 嶼, which
invariably denotes an island (of no great size), is
followed in the translation by preserving in all
cases the word *Shan* where it occurs in the names
of localities given.

† 句欄山, the most patient research has
failed to discover the exact whereabouts of this
point, but from all the data obtained, it would
seem to lie somewhere on the western coast of
Borneo. It is undoubtedly the same with Kiao-
lan Shan 交欄山, of which mention will be
found further on. In support of the view taken
respecting its probable situation, reference may
be made to the *Sing-ch'a*, in which it is stated
that "the cluster of islands called Kia-li-ma-ting
假里馬丁 lie opposite to Kiao-lan Shan."
In the Chronicle of the Yüan dynasty the name
is written 假里馬荅, Ka-li-ma-ta. This
group can be no other than the Carimata Islands,
lying between Borneo and Billiton (or Britung).
The last named would appear to be the large
island described in the same work as Ma-(Ba)-
yih-tung 麻逸凍, where it is said to lie to
the southwest of Kiao-lan Shan. If this identi-

water may be procured, and thirty watches
farther on lies Ki-li-mên-shan.* Beyond
this, a distance of five watches, is Hu-ts'iao-
shan,† and three watches farther on is Na-
ts'au-shan,‡ from which point Tu-pan may
be reached. In four watches more the
vessel reaches Sin-ts'un§ in Kwa-wa. The
capital city is named Man-chê-peh-i.‖—*Obs.*
Man-chê-peh-i is the name of a place where
foreign vessels congregate. One arrives first
at Tu-che,¶ then at Sin-ts'un, next at Su-
lu-ma-yih,** and afterwards at the residence
of the King. In the chapter on Kwa-wa in

fication be correct, Kiao-lan Shan would lie somewhere in the neighbourhood of the present settlement of Pontianak.

* 吉里門山, this point there is no difficulty in identifying with Pulo Krimun, or
Carimon Java, a small group of islands, lying
immediately opposite the northernmost headland
of Java. The same name occurs also in other
parts of the Archipelago, and is applied moreover
to a portion of the coast of Borneo, of which, according to Knight's *Cyclopædia of Geography*,
"the native name is Kalamantin."

† 胡椒山, Pepper Headland or Mountain.
This would appear, from the above and other
data, to be Tanjong Buang, as the northernmost
headland of Java is called on Crawfurd's map.

‡ 那參山, this may also be read Na-shên.
Its proximity to Tupan (Tuban) and to the Strait
of Madura identifies this locality with the cape
marked Tanjong Uwer Uwer of Crawfurd's map.

§ 新村, *i.e.* New Town. This appears to
have been a settlement founded by the early Chinese colonists, at the entrance to the Strait of
Madura, in the neighbourhood of Gresik.

‖ 滿者伯夷, there can be no doubt
that this sound is intended to represent Modjopahit, the name of one of the ancient States of
the island, with reference to which Crawfurd
gives the following particulars: "The origin of
the last and best known of the Hindu states of
Java, Mojopahit, remains as undetermined as
that of Pajajaran. . . . All accounts agree that
Mojopahit was destroyed in the year of Salivana
1400, or 1478 of Christ, and from presumptive
evidence it is inferred that it may have been
founded about a century and a half before. The
dynasty of princes which reigned at Mojopahit
appears to have extended its authority over the
finest provinces of the island" (*Hist. Ind. Archipel.*, II., p. 301).

¶ The character 枝 in the text is doubtless a
block-cutter's error for 板 pan, the name being
Tu-pan, as stated lower down.

** 蘇魯馬益, Surabaya.

the Annals of the Yüan dynasty, it is stated that the Pa-tsich-(tsit) channel 八 節 澗 leads to Tu-ma-pan 杜 馬 班, the King's residence. This the interpreters have erroneously represented as Tu-pan 杜 板. —There are no walled cities in this country. The King's palace is surrounded with lofty walls, with gateways one within the other. The buildings are in shape like towers, and are roofed with planks of wood. The custom is to sit upon mats.—*Obs.* The walls are upwards of three *chang* in height (=about 40 feet), and they are built of brick. They are two hundred and odd paces in circuit.* Planks of hard wood are used instead of tiles. The palace is very elegantly adorned. For every three or four persons a board is laid down, upon which fine mats of rattan are spread, and on these people take their seats, crosslegged.—The habitations of the common people are covered with a thatch of leaves. For the storage of articles of every description they use receptacles like chests, made of brick, three or four feet high, and upon these the natives sit or lie down to sleep. The King wears his hair gathered up on the head, and sometimes he puts on a crown adorned with leaves of gold. He wears no clothing on the upper part of his person, and his feet are likewise bare. From the waist downwards he wears a garment†

* This is a statement borrowed, with other particulars, from the *Ying Yai*, where, however, the dimensions given are one hundred and odd paces, and are probably meant to refer to the royal residence 王 之 所 居 which is spoken of as enclosed within the walls. Crawfurd states that "The walls of the most ancient *Kāratons* (or palaces) were constructed of hewn stone. They were afterwards constructed of an excellent fabric of mortar, as at Mojopahit. . . . Of the extent of these walled cities we may form some notion by that of the modern one of the Sultan of Java, which is three miles round, and contains a population of ten thousand inhabitants, the largest of all was Mojopahit." (*Hist. Ind. Archipel.*, I., p. 165).

† 幔, properly speaking a scarf. By this, undoubtedly, the *Sarong* is intended, of which Crawfurd gives the following description: " The *Sarong* . . is a piece of cloth, generally coloured, six or eight feet long, and three or four feet wide, usually sewed at both ends. This sort of petti-

embroidered with silk; and the waist is wrapped round with a satin sash. He wears a dagger* by his side, to which the name of *Pu ts'ze t'ow*† is given. When he goes abroad, he rides upon an elephant or in a chariot drawn by oxen. He has eight ministers. Of the natives, the men wear their hair gathered in a knot, and carry daggers.—*Obs.* From the time a child reaches the age of three, every one, whether rich or poor, has the *pu ts'ze t'ow* by his side. These weapons are invariably of the very finest steel,‡ of the "rabbit hair" or "snow coat, which is common to both sexes, is of the same breadth above and below, and is not secured to the body by any permanent contrivance, but the upper part being contracted to the size of the waist, the superfluous portion, as occasion requires, is twisted with the hand, and tucked in between the rest of the garment and the body of the wearer." (*Hist. Ind. Archipel.*, I., p. 209).

* 刃, lit. a sharp-pointed weapon, doubtless the well-known *Kris* or dagger of the Malay race. Cf. Crawfurd, (*His. Ind. Archipel.*, I., pp. 224-226).

† 不 刺 頭, lit. "Strike not at the head." According to Crawfurd (II., p. 349), "spears, cannon, and krises are frequently particularized by name." The character 刺 *la*, however, in M. Schlegel's version, substituted for 刺, *ts'ze*, as in the text, has led him to read the name as *pu-la-t'ow*, a combination to which it is difficult to assign a meaning. The great degree of reverence for the head, mentioned farther on in the text, appears sufficiently to account for the name given to the *kris* as above stated.

‡ 鑌 鐵—*Pin-t'ieh*. This is defined in K'ang-hi's Dictionary as simply signifying "good iron, of which swords are made." The article is mentioned among the products brought from Arabia to China under the Sung dynasty. Julien was of opinion that the diamond was understood by this term—for what reason it is not easy to conceive. Cf. *Mélanges de Géographie Asiatique*, (I., p. 91), quoted by Dr. Bretschneider in his pamphlet " *On the Knowledge possessed by the Ancient Chinese of the Arabs and Arabian Colonies and other Western Countries*," p. 12. In the *P'ei Wên Yün Fu* the character *pin* is written without the radical " iron," and the following passages are quoted as authorities for the words: (1°). "In the country of Kao Ch'ang (the land of the Uigurs), there is a kind of grit-stone 礪 石, from which, when it is broken open, *pin-t'ieh* is obtained. To this the name 'iron-eating stone ' is given." *Chronicle of the Sung Dynasty.—Chapter on Foreign Countries).—*(2°). " The nation of the Liao took the name of *Pin T'ieh* as their

flake" temper. The handles are of gold, or of rhinoceros horn or ivory, and engraved with figures of men or other objects.—The women wear their hair in a knot, and are clothed in a short vest covering the upper part of the person, with a *sarong* below the waist. Both men and women are very particular in the regard they cherish for the head. If any one receive a blow in that part, he instantly draws his dagger to stab the offender.

Flogging or bastinadoing is not practised in this country. The only punishment inflicted is that of death. This is the way they execute. The victim's hands are bound behind his back with rattans: he is driven forward a few steps, and then stabbed. * If one who has slain another man keep out

designation, in allusion to its quality of hardness. Yet, *pin-t'ieh*, hard though it be, in time becomes subject to decay. The only thing that will not perish by decay is gold (kin—金). For this reason, the title of KIN was adopted for the state." (*Chronicle of the Liao dynasty.—History of T'ai Tsu,* the founder of the dynasty).— (3 °). "The diamond borer perforates the jadestone: the sword of *pin-t'ieh* will [sever] the floating down." (*Poems of Yüan Chén*—flourished A.D. 779-831). It seems probable that the finely-tempered metal thus extolled was the same with the *Ondanique* or *Andaine,* the Indian steel, respecting which Colonel Yule has a highly instructive note (*Marco Polo,* II., chap. xvii). In the same way as Avicenna, according to Roger Bacon, quoted by Colonel Yule, distinguishes three different species of iron, the third of which is *Andena,* so the author of the *Pên Ts'ao Kang Muh,* writing in the 16th century, declares that there are three kinds of steel 鋼鐵. The method of manufacturing two of these is described. The third is said to be "naturally produced among the islands of the Southern ocean, and to resemble the amethyst in form." All sharp-edged weapons, axes, and chisels are made, it is added, of this steel. (本草鋼目, B. 8).

* The particulars here given are strikingly in accord with the statements made by Crawfurd respecting the laws in force among the Javanese. Cf. *Hist. Ind. Archipel.,* III., p. 105. The concise details of the text are abridged in the most ruthless manner from the much fuller account given in the *Ying Yai,* where the manner of giving the death-blow by a stab in the region of the abdomen is described. The author adds: "Not a day passes in this country without some one's life being taken—a dreadful state of matters, in good sooth."

of the way for three days, he is pardoned; but if taken on the spot, he is put to death.

At Tu-pan, there are some thousand or more of the natives *(fan jên)* living. The water near Tu-pan is known by the name of *Shéng shui* (Holy Water).—*Obs.* In the Annals of the Yüan dynasty this place is called Tu-ma-pan. A headman of the barbarians is governor there. Among the inhabitants there are numbers of emigrants 流戶 from Kwangtung and Chang Chow [in China]. Near the sea-shore there is a lake, respecting which the natives relate that when the generals of the Yüan dynasty, She Pih and Kao Hing,* invaded Java, they were kept from landing for a whole month and ran short of water. The two generals made prayer to Heaven, upon which a fountain of sweet water burst forth: and hence it has received the name of Holy Water.—The number of inhabitants at Sin Ts'un is about one thousand and upwards. Another name of the place is Keh-'rh-si Yüan.†—*Obs.* Travelling eastward from Tu-pan one comes in half a day's journey to Keh-'rh-si Yüan, which was originally [named] Ku T'an 古灘. The people of the country having established a settlement here, it received the name of Sin Ts'un (New Town). The King of the town is a native of Kwangtung. Here the foreign shipping all congregates, and merchandize of every description is stored. The people of the place are very wealthy. Their houses are covered with woven *Kadjang* leaves, and the shops and places of trade joined in rows form a market. —At Su-lu-ma-yih (Surabaya) there are a thousand or more households. The place is also called Su-'rh-pa-ya.—*Obs.* In one day's journey southward from Sin Ts'un one arrives at a shallow harbour (or stream), and the place is reached by a journey of 30 odd *li* (about 12 miles) in small boats.—Here

* See Note III. at foot.

† 革兒昔原. The third character would be sounded in Southern Chinese as *sik*, and the name would seem to signify the plain (*Yüan*) of Keh'rhsik, by which no doubt Gresik or Garsik near Surabaya is denoted.

are multitudes of apes, to which women who are desirous of conceiving offer up prayers. —*Obs.* There is an island in the harbour which is densely overgrown with trees, and in this forest some ten thousand long-tailed apes have their habitation. An old black male ape is their chief, and he is followed by an old native (or savage 番) woman. Women who are childless carry offerings of wine, victuals, fruit, and flowers, which they present with supplications to the old ape. If he be pleased, he eats of the offerings, and his followers devour the remainder. After this a male and female ape come out before them and copulate. The woman, on returning home, becomes with child. If the offerings are not eaten and the ceremony fulfilled, the woman will not become pregnant. The local tradition is to the effect that during the period of the T'ang dynasty some five thousand of the inhabitants, being in a state of destitution, were visited by a priest who wielded supernatural powers, and who transformed them into apes. Only one old woman was left unchanged in shape. Their dwellings still exist. In the Annals of the Sung dynasty it is stated that the mountains abound in apes, which have no fear of man. When summoned with a sound resembling the words *siao-siao* they will come forth, and if fruits be offered to them two of their company will come forward first. These are called by the natives the monkey King and Queen. When they have eaten their fill the others come and help themselves. In this account, nothing is said about women becoming with child.—

At Man-ehê-peh-i there are some 300 households.—*Obs.* By travelling for 70 or 80 *li* in a small boat from Su-'rh-pa-ya one reaches a town which the natives call Chang-ku 漳沽. Landing here, a day-and-a-half's journey brings one [to Modjopahit].— At this place the people sleep without pillows, and in eating they use neither spoons nor chopsticks. At their meals, having rinsed their mouths and hands, they gather

in a circle, when platters of butter and rice are set before them, which they take up with the fingers. They drink water, and [chew] areca-nut with the betel leaf and chunam (shell lime). In their entertainment of guests the proceeding is the same.

Among the inhabitants of this country there are but three classes, namely, the Mohammedans *(hwei-hwei)*, Chinese *(T'ang jên)*,* and the natives *(t'u jên)*. The Mohammedans are descendants of the foreign traders from different parts, who have taken up their residence here. They cultivate elegance and daintiness in their apparel and way of living. The natives are repulsive in aspect and black in colour. Their heads are monkey-like in shape, and they go barefoot. Their religion is the worship of demons, and they use as food all manner of unclean things, such as serpents, ants, and worms, which they devour after scorching them over a fire.† They take their food and lie down to sleep together with their dogs.

There [was formerly] in this country a supernatural occurrence [called that of] "the rogue elephant" 閣象.‡ In all their let-

---

* See foot note, *ante*, Part III. (*China Review*, Vol. IV. No. 2, 1875, p. 62).

† Cf. Crawfurd: "In the Níti Sástra of the Javanese there is a passage which recommends to *persons of rank* not to eat dogs, rats, snakes, lizards, and caterpillars. The practice of using these disgusting animals as food must have been frequent, or the injunction were unnecessary." (*Hist. Ind. Archipel.*, II., p. 233.)

‡ This statement would be unintelligible without a reference to the *Ying Yai*, which gives the following as an ancient legend of the country: "It happened that a Mâra Râja, son of the devils, who had a blue face, a red body, and scarlet hair, united himself here with a rogue elephant. From this union more than one hundred sons were born, whose custom it was to drink blood and to devour men's bodies. Many were those devoured by them, until of a sudden, one day, a thunderbolt struck a rock and split it open, when a man was discovered seated within. All were astonished at this sight, and they hailed him as king. Upon this he caused a valiant army to drive out the progeny of the rogue elephant, and to do no harm to the people, who increased and multiplied in peace thereafter."

The *Mâra Râja*, in Chinese 魔王, of the text is the arch-enemy who plays so prominent a part in Sanskrit and especially Buddhist literature. He "is often represented with one hundred arms

ters between officials they use the date 1376.*
—*Obs.* This would make their era commence with the period of the Western Han
in China.—In their calendar, the year
begins with the tenth moon. In this moon,
the sovereign rides abroad in a lofty chariot,
and presides at the feast of lances.—*Obs.*
In proceeding to the place of entertainment,
the sovereign's female consorts go first, and
he follows behind. They ride in tower-like
carriages, more than a *chang* (11 feet) high,
borne on two wheels, and with windows on
four sides. These carriages are drawn by
horses. The men of the country come with
their wives, and are drawn up in ranks,
holding in their hands bamboos pointed to
form spears. The women are armed with
staves three feet long. They advance to
combat at the sound of a drum, and desist
at a given signal. The encounter takes place
three times in succession. The women attack with their staves. When *na-ts'ze, na-
ts'ze*, is called out, they fall back. Whoever
kills an opponent is held to be victor. The
victor gives a piece of gold to the family of
the man he has slain, and takes to himself
his wife.†

At the marriage ceremony among this
people, the union takes place at the house of
the bride, who, after three days have elapsed,
removes with her husband to his abode. On
the way, she is met by musicians, and she
is conveyed to her new home in a gaily-
decorated boat.‡ The bridegroom's parents

and riding on an elephant" (Eitel, *Hand-book of
Chinese Buddhism*, p. 73).
* See Note IV. at foot.
† This festival, mentioned in the account supplied to M. Schlegel, is stated by him, in a foot
note, to be "Kharblijkelijk het Jav. *Séninan* of
Steekspel" (p. 17); but I have not been able to
meet with any description of the performance referred to. In many details, however, the account
given in the text corresponds with the minute
description of the festivals in which the Javanese
delight, given by Crawfurd (*Hist. Ind. Archipel.*, II., p. 262-264). The introduction of
Mohammedanism has done little, it is remarked,
toward modifying the ancient customs, derived
from India, in this respect.
‡ Cf. Raffles, *Hist. of Java.* "At sunset on
the wedding day, the bridegroom went in proces-
sion to visit the parents of the bride, after which

go to meet the bride, with beating of kettle-
drums and gongs and blowing of calabash-
horns. The [bride and bridegroom are]
surrounded by persons with fire-tubes,* short
swords, and circular shields. The bride
wears her hair gathered in a knot, the upper
part of her person uncovered and her feet
bare. Below the waist she is clad in an
embroidered *sarong*. On her neck she wears
a collar of gold and pearls, with bracelets
upon her arms. The relations, friends, and
neighbours deck the marrirge-boat with
betel leaves and garlands of flowers, and in
this wise escort her home. A feast lasting
several days is then indulged in.

she was visited by his parents. Five days after
the consecration of the marriage the parents of
the bride, with whom she staid for that period,
prepared a feast." I. p. 363. Again: "Among the
people termed *Kálang*, (an aboriginal race), the
married couple lived in the house of the bride's
father till the third day," p. 366. Crawfurd says:
"All the native ceremonies are solemnized at the
house of the bride's father. The bride and
bridegroom, with their friends, parade the country, village, or town, attended by music, decorated in their gayest attire, and decked with the
borrowed jewels of the best part of the neighbourhood. The bridegroom is always mounted.
The bride is conducted in a kind of open litter.
(*Hist. Ind. Archipel.*, I., p. 91).
* This a noteworthy passage, if by the expression fire-tube 火銃, used in the text, the dis-
charge of gun-powder be implied. The original
authority upon which the above passage is based
is the *Ying Yai*, where the statement is even
more explicit, the expression employed being
放火銃 *letting off fire-tubes.* As the author
of this work, Ma Hwan, dates his preface in
A.D. 1416, and gives 1413 as the year in which
he accompanied the eunuch Chêng Ho on his
voyage, the period at which fire-arms would seem
to have been known among the Javanese is fixed
with tolerable certainty. Crawfurd, indeed, as-
serts that "the use of small arms the Indian
islanders *undoubtedly* acquired from the Europeans. The matchlock they call by its Portuguese name, the firelock by a Dutch, and the
pistol by a Dutch or English one. The matchlock was not employed in Europe for ten years
after the Portuguese conquered Malacca (A.D.
1511); so that, if Europeans had observed the
use of it among the islanders, they could not
have failed to notice so extraordinary a fact, when
so frequently engaged in hostilities with them."
(*Hist. Ind. Archipel.*, I., p. 228). In immediate
juxtaposition with this remark, however, Crawfurd observes that "it is possible that the East
Indian islanders were not indebted to the European nations for this first knowledge of fire-
arms, but may have acquired it in the course of

Three methods are followed in disposing of the dead. One is cremation; the other casting into the water; and the third leaving the body to be devoured by dogs.* Wives and concubines are greatly addicted to the practice of self-destruction on a husband's death.†—*Obs.* When parents are about to die, the children enquire of them what their last wishes are. If the dying person express a desire to be devoured after death by the dogs, the body is cast out into the fields, and if it be wholly devoured the survivors rejoice thereat; but, if otherwise, there is grief and lamentation, and the remains are cast into the sea. When the wives and concubines of principal persons devote themselves to death in fulfilment of a vow on the decease of their lords, a scaffolding is formed of wood, about which fuel is heaped, and at the proper moment the women, their hair decked with ornaments and flowers, and wearing robes of many colours, throw themselves weeping into the flames and are consumed together.—

their commerce with China." In an enquiry on the Introduction and Use of Gunpowder and Fire-arms among the Chinese (*Journal of the North China Branch of the Royal Asiatic Society*, Shanghai, 1871), the writer has already shewn that, as a propulsive agent, gunpowder was not in use among the Chinese before the early part of the 15th century, but that in the invasion of Tonquin in 1407 the natives of that region were found employing tubes filled with inflammable material for purposes of warfare. In this paper, it has been suggested (p. 95), that the embassies which were sent by the Emperor Yung Loh to almost every part of southern and western Asia may have been the means by which China became possessed of the secret of the use of gunpowder in its most efficacious form of application. With the statement of Ma Hwan before us, there can be little doubt that in the very beginning of the 15th century, fire-arms of some description were in the hands of the people of Java.

* This is in exact correspondence with the description given by Raffles: "There were three modes of disposing of the body of a deceased person before Mohammedanism was introduced: by fire, termed *óbong*; by water, termed *lárung*; or by exposing it upright against a tree in a forest, where it was left to decay, termed *setra*." (*Hist. of Java*, I., p. 364).

† See Crawfurd's account of the prevalence of sutteeism in the island of Bali, where, he states, "the practice is carried to an excess unknown even to India herself." (*Hist. Ind. Archipel.*, II., p. 241).

The people are wealthy. In their commerce they make use of Chinese copper *cash* of successive reigns of the past. The chief products of the soil are rice and pulse. Two crops are gathered yearly. The six kinds of domestic animals (*i.e.* the horse, the ox, the sheep or goat, the pig, the dog, and the domestic fowl) are reared among them. Their writing they form by incisions with a knife on *Kadjang* leaves. The written character resembles that of So-li.* Touching their weights: 2 *fên* 2 *li* make one *kupang*, and 4 *kupang* make 1 *ts'ien*: sixteen *ts'ien* make 1 *liang*, and 20 *liang* make one *kin*.† Their measures of length are formed of segments of bamboo. Of measures of capacity, that which answers to the Chinese *shêng* is called *kula*, and holds 1 *shêng* 8 *koh*; and their *tow* is called *nali*, holding 8 *shêng*.‡

The women of the country are used to sing in the public roads on the night of the full moon. Their voices are sweet and tender.—*Obs.* At these times of song, the

* 鎮 俚. By the name of So-li, the inhabitants of the Malay Archipelago appear to have designated the Southern portion of the Indian Peninsula, to which, indeed, the same name is given by Marco Polo. The Venetian traveller speaks of "the Kingdom of Maabar called So-li, which is the best and noblest province of India." (Yule's *Marco Polo*, 1st. ed. II., p. 299). Colonel Yule is of opinion that, almost beyond a doubt, So-li is the same with Chola or Soladesam, *i.e.* Tanjore (p. 272, *note*). Chulia is at the present day a common designation for the natives of Southern India, or their descendants, in the Malay islands. The derivation of the Javanese written character from the Sanskrit alphabet is well-known (See Crawfurd, *Hist. Ind. Archipel.*, II., p. 3).

† This corresponds with the weights in use in Achin, (Sumatra), as given in Prinsep's *Useful Tables*, Part I., p. 80. The "tale" of 16 mace (*liang*) is there said to be equal to 64 copangs, precisely as above indicated. Crawfurd says: "In Achin, the greatest of all the commercial states of the Archipelago, five *tahils* made a *bungkal*, and twenty *bungkals* one *kati*" (*Hist. Ind. Archipel.*, 1., p. 283). The value of the *kati* (catty) at Achin is given by Prinsep as 2 lb. 1 oz. 14¼ drs. avoirdupois. It differs therefore from the Chinese *kin* (catty) of 1¼ lb., containing 16 *liang* (*taels*) of 10 *ts'ien* (*mace*) each.

‡ The four measures actually in common use among the Chinese are the *koh* 合, the *shêng* 升, the half-*shêng*, and the *tow* 斗. The three

native women gather joyously in bands of twenty or thirty, having one person as their leader. She, with waving arms and measured paces, chants one of the melodies of the people. After each verse the whole company raise their voices together in chorus. Presents of money and other things are given them as they pass the doors of friends or kinsfolk.—

The people draw pictures and assemble together to interpret their meaning.—*Obs.* Figures of human beings, birds, beasts, and fishes are drawn upon paper in the form of a scroll, the roller* of which is of wood, three feet in length. People seat themselves in a circle on the ground and unroll the drawings, the meaning of which is explained in a loud voice; and bystanders gather around to listen to the merry tale.—

The climate is one of unchanging warmth. Among the productions of the country there are sappan-wood in abundance, diamonds, white sandal-wood, cardamoms, steel (*pin-t'ieh*—see previous Note), tortoise-shell, many red and green birds of the parrot kind,

first are made of the cylindrical joints of the bamboo; and the *tow* is made of wood in the shape of the frustum of a pyramid. There are two sizes of the *tow* and *shêng*; one, called 十斤斗 or ten-catty *tow*, contains precisely that quantity of rice, and the *shêng*, one-tenth of the *tow*, is made to hold one catty. The second size, called the 倉斗 or granary *tow*, holds about six and a half catties of rice. The corresponding *shêng* contains 30.43415 cubic inches, and is therefore about one-sixth less than the English pint. Ten *hoh* make one *shêng*. See Bridgman's *Chinese Chrestomathy*, p. 383. The Javanese measure equivalent to a gallon is said by Crawfurd to be called by some tribes a *kulak.* (*Hist. Ind. Archipel.*, I., p. 273).

* The whole of this passage, as also the foregoing details with reference to the manners and customs of the Javanese, is obviously transferred from the *Ying Yai*, the plain and circumstantial language of which, however, is absurdly travestied in the compiler's pedantic anxiety for literary elegance. Instead of a "roller" 軸, as stated in the text, the eye-witness from whose record the description is transferred says that "two posts three feet high are planted in the ground to suspend the pictures upon, and the exhibitor squats on the ground beside them to deliver his narration." This is doubtless one of the "professed story-tellers" of whom Crawfurd speaks.

pearl-fowls, love-birds, peacocks, areca-nut sparrows, pearl and green doves, white deer in great numbers, and white monkeys.* Plantains grow abundantly, and there are also sugar-cane, pomegranates, nelumbium seed-vessels, and vegetables of the love-apple and melon kind. There is one kind of fruit, in shape like the pomegranate, with a thick rind and white pulp, called the *mang-ki-she.*† Another, resembling in shape the *p'i-pa* (*loquat eribotrya*), contains a very delicious white pulp, and is called *lung-ch'a.*‡ There is also a plant, the leaf of which is like the · *kü* 蒟 (betel pepper), and its stalk like a slender stem of bamboo. It flowers in Spring, and produces a fruit like the mulberry, but closer and smaller. The name of this is *pi-po.*§ When eaten, it cures internal congestions; and its root is a specific against swellings.

A turtle is found here, which has a head

* According to Raffles, "of the parrot-kind, two only, the *bétet* and *selindit*, are found in Java. The peacock is very common in large forests. Two varieties of the turtle are found in the seas surrounding Java. Both yield the substance called tortoise-shell." (*Hist. of Java*, I. pp. 57, 59). The birds designated as "pearl fowl" and "areca-nut sparrows" in the Chinese text I am unable positively to identify. The 倒掛鳥 is identified by Swinhoe with the *loriculus paniculus* or Love Bird. Its Chinese appellation, based upon its habit of hanging head downwards, he translates topsy-turvy hanger. See *Birds and Beasts of Formosa*, in Journal N. C. B. R. As. Society, Vol. II., p. 46.

† 恭吉柿. This is evidently the mangostin, (*Garcinia mangostana*), called *Manggis*, or *Manggusta* by the natives of the Archipelago. Crawfurd says of it: "In external appearance it has the look of a ripe pomegranate, but is smaller, and more completely globular. A rind something hard on the outside, but soft and succulent within, encloses large seeds or kernels, surrounded by a soft, semi-transparent snow-white pulp, now and then having a very slight crimson blush. This pulp is the edible part of the fruit." (*Hist. Ind. Archipel.*, I., p. 417).

‡ 郎极. This may perhaps be the *langseh*, described by Crawfurd, Vol. I., p. 432. The character *Ch'a* 极, given in the *Ying Yai*, is erroneously written *pan* 板 in the text.

§ 華撥. The long Pepper (*Chavica Roxburghii*). Cf. F. P. Smith's *Chin. Mat. Med.*, p. 138.

and snout like a parrot's beak. It has a large mouth and rounded back. Its scales, which are covered with red spots and markings, are called *tai-mei*,* and they serve if worn on the person as a charm against witchcraft and poison. [Near Java] there is a mountain, very lofty and of great extent, called Kiao-lan,† which abounds in leopards. The natives make hunting with bows and arrows their occupation.—*Obs.* According to what is related, when the generals Kao-Hing and She Pih led their expedition against Java, they landed at this place to build some ships, and they left behind them some hundred or more of their sick, whose progeny has increased and multiplied here.—

Bordering upon Java there lies the [island] called Chung-ka-lo,‡ in which there are lofty mountains and rocks of beautiful shape.

* 瑇瑁. The scales of the *Chelonia imbricata* or hawk's-bill turtle, commonly found in the seas of the Archipelago.

† 交欄 Kiao, or Kao, Lan. This, it is evident, is the same with the Kew Lan 句欄 spoken of at the commencement of the present section, as lying 30 watches from Carimon Java, and identified conjecturally with a point on the coast of Borneo. In the *Sing Ch'a* a separate description is devoted to this locality, which is said to lie at a distance of ten days' sail, with a fair wind, from Ling Shan on the coast of Cochin China, whilst Surabaya is said, in the same work, to be 20 days' sail from that headland. It is further stated that the expedition under the Mongol leaders was driven by stress of weather to Kiao-lan, and that, a large portion of the fleet being disabled, it was necessary to build no less than 100 vessels here, in order to continue the voyage to Java. The adjacent forests are represented as producing all materials requisite for shipbuilding. In the Chronicle of the Yüan dynasty the name is written 勾闌—Kow-lan.

‡ 重迦羅. The compiler here draws his information from the *Sing Ch'a*, in which, however, no indication is given as to the whereabouts of the locality described. This omission can be repaired by reference to the Chinese sailing directions, dating from the early part of the 17th century, which have already been made use of for the coast of Cochin China (See Vol. III., p. 322). In this work a course is laid down, starting from Gresik 吉力石港, which is described as a town in the district of Tupan, and proceeding first E. by S. and then S. W. by S. to

Beneath one of the mountains there is a cavern, which is so large that ten thousand men would find room within. The natives here make salt by boiling sea-water, and they distil spirits from grain. Antelopes abound here, and parrots. The tree-cotton * and cocoa-nut tree are cultivated. From this point, at a distance of several days' sail, there lie the following places: Sunt'o-lo; P'i-pa-she; Tan Ch'ung; Yüan K'iao; and P'êng-li.† The natives live by piracy, and hold intercourse with the kingdoms of Ki-t'o-k'i. It is seldom that trading-vessels are able to go near them.

Mo-li Shan 磨里山, which it is observed is the same with the P'êng-li Shan 彭里山 mentioned in the *Sing Ch'a Shêng Lan*. This, it is evident, is the island of Bali, immediately contiguous to Java on the east. Next comes Lang-muk 郎木, or Lombok, and beyond this Sam-ba-wa 三吧哇. The next point steered from, five watches distant from Lombok, is said to be Chung-ka-lo, which would seem, therefore, to be the island of Floris; and five watches farther lies Volcano Island, 火山, a term which would apply to almost any island of this group. The great cavern mentioned in the text may perhaps have been the crater of some extinct volcano.

* 木棉. This term was most probably used to denote the true cotton plant, so largely cultivated in the islands of the Archipelago. As the writer has elsewhere shewn, the plant received this appellation in Southern China on its introduction from the countries farther south, probably at some time during the 10th century, the name being borrowed from the cotton tree or *Bombax*, with obvious reference to the silky down produced by that tree (See *Notes and Queries on China and Japan*, Vol. II., 1868, p. 73).

† The following are the Chinese characters employed for the names given above: 1. 孫陀羅;—2. 琵琶施;—3. 丹重;—4. 圓嶠;—5. 彭里. The third and fourth have less the appearance of native names, phonetically rendered, than of purely, Chinese designations. The fifth, as explained in the note above, is intended for Bali. By the "Kingdoms of Ki-t'o-k'i" 吉陀崎諸國" it is possible that Celebes, with its singular peninsular formation, may be referred to. The passage rendered above "at the distance of several days' sail" is, in the text: 其山下水程有五 (*lit.* from

There are no fixed seasons for sending tribute from Java. In the third year of Hung Wu (A. D. 1370) the Sovereign, named Si-li-pa-ta-la (Sri Badra?) sent one of his officers named Pa-ti-chen-pi and others to offer tribute of productions of the country, and to give back two edicts which had been bestowed by the Yüan dynasty. In 1381 the King sent an address written on leaves of gold, together with tribute, and also three hundred black slaves.[*] After this, tribute was broken off. In 1404 the King of Yüan Tung (*lit.* East Garden) sent an envoy with tribute, and begged that a seal be given to him. Upon this it was decreed that a silver seal should be cast, and plated with gold, and this was sent by the hands of an envoy. In 1443 it was arranged

this island there are five journeys by water); but this scarcely intelligible passage is a garbled version of the text of the *Sing Ch'a*, where, with perfect distinctness, it is stated that 其 處 約 去 數 日 水 程; and this reading has been followed in the translation.

[*] The following is extracted from a note on this subject communicated by the writer to *Notes and Queries on China and Japan* for July, 1869 (Vol. III., No. 7): "The fact of negro slavery having at one time been numbered among the institutions of China is not generally known. The work entitled 粵 中 見 聞, a valuable repertory of notices relating to the province of Kwangtung, states as follows under the heading 黑 人—Black Men: 'During the most prosperous times of the Ming dynasty large numbers of black men were purchased by the great houses at Canton to serve as gatekeepers. The name given to them was 鬼 奴—devil slave—and their strength was most extraordinary, to such an extent that they were capable of carrying a weight of several hundred catties on their backs. In language, habits, and inclinations there was no similarity between them and the natives of China; but in disposition they were tractable and not given to running away. In colour they were black as ink, with red lips and white teeth, their hair curly and of a yellow hue. They were of both the male and female sex, and were produced among the islands beyond the sea, where they lived on raw food. When caught, and fed on a diet cooked with fire, they were attacked with violent and long-continued purging, which was called "changing their inwards," and in many cases the result was death. Those who did not die could be kept in captivity for a length of time, and were capable of being taught to understand ordinary speech, although they

that tribute should be sent every third year; but since then it has not been sent with regularity. The tribute that was sent was of pepper; long pepper; sappan wood; bees' wax; catechu; diamonds; ebony; native red earth (?); rose-water; lign aloes; sandal wood; *ma-t'êng hiang*: *suh hiang*: laka wood; putchuk; olibanum; Baroos camphor; dragon's blood; nutmegs; cardamoms; *t'êng kieh*: assa-fœtida; aloes; myrrh; lucrabau seeds; clove bark; native *mah pieh tsze*: vermin-destroying preparation; pottery stone; cubebs; *wu hiang*; precious stones; pearls; tin; iron from the western seas; iron weapons; wrought-iron knives; *mi* cloth; glazed red cloth (calicoes); peacocks; fire birds;[*] parrots; tortoise-shell; peacock-feathers; kingfisher feathers; themselves were not able to talk. There was one variety who, diving into the sea, would remain under water for one or two days. These were called Kw'ên-lun Nu 崑 崙 奴, and during the period of the T'ang dynasty they were kept in large numbers by families of distinction and wealthy houses.'" In the curious little work called the 海 島 逸 誌, by Wang Ta-hai, published about A.D. 1791, and translated under the title of "The Chinaman Abroad" (Mission Press, Shanghai, 1849), the black slaves which were owned in Java in the middle of the last century, and which are described as being natives of Papua and Ceram, are amusingly noticed. It is said that they were called 烏 鬼 or black demons. In connection with the fact that these Papuan blackamoors were not unnaturally called "devils" by the Cantonese of the 15th and 16th centuries, as stated in the extract quoted above, may not the ill-famed appellation 番 鬼—foreign devil—with which Europeans have so long been saluted in the south of China have owed its origin to the currency of this nickname? The transfer would have been easy and almost natural, from one class of "foreigner" to another.

[*] In its description of Palembang (in Sumatra) the *Ying Yai* describes the 火 鷄 or "fire bird" as follows: "It is a bird as tall as the Manchurian crane 仙 鶴, with a round body, an upright neck longer even than the crane's, a soft red crest like a red cap, and two wattles on the neck. Its beak is pointed. The plumage over its whole body is like sheep's wool, loose, long, and of a dark 青 colour. Its feet are long, and iron-black in colour. Its claws are very sharp, so that if it strikes a man in the belly it tears out his entrails and kills him. It is fond

cranes' crests ; * rhinoceros-horns ; tusks of ivory ; turtle shells ; prepared lign-aloes ; and gum benzoin.†

EPILOGUE :—In the reign Ch'un Hwa (A.D. 990-994) an envoy from this country named T'o-chan 陀湛 declared himself, saying,—In China there has come to reign a true lord over men ; and upon this an embassy was fitted forth and offerings of tribute were despatched. The Mongol who reigned under the title of Yüan 胡元 sent She Pih and Kao Hing with a fleet of a thousand sail, bearing victuals for a whole year, and invested with ten warrants of command in the shape of "tiger" staves, with forty

of eating live coals, and hence it is called the fire bird." In this description it is easy to recognize the cassowary, which, at the present day, according to Wallace, inhabits the island of Ceram only. He describes it as follows: "It is a stout and strong bird, standing five or six feet high, and covered with long coarse hair-like feathers. The head is ornamented with a large horny casque or helmet, and the bare skin of the neck is conspicuous with bright blue and red colours... This bird is the *Casuarius Galeatus* of naturalists, and was for a long time the only species known. Others have since been discovered in New Guinea, New Britain, and North Australia." (*The Malay Archipelago*, Vol. II., p. 149). The cassowary, when attacked, defends itself by kicking obliquely backwards with its feet, (*Chambers's Cyclopædia*). The name *hwo-ki* 火鶏 or "fire fowl," by which the turkey is now known in Southern China, may not improbably have been given to it from some general resemblance to the cassowary of the Indian islands, on its first introduction to the knowledge of the Chinese.
* The *Ying Yai* gives the following description of the substance referred to: " The cranes'-crest bird 崔頂鳥 is of the size of a duck, with black plumage, a long neck, and a large beak. The bone of its skull is more than an inch in thickness. It is red on the outside and like yellow wax within, presenting a most beautiful and delicate appearance. The name given to it is cranes'-crest; and it is used for making dagger handles, clasps, and the like." The bird thus described is doubtless the great Hornbill (*Buceros*), belonging to a family abundantly represented in the islands of the Archipelago. The fine drawing of a specimen of *Buceros bicornis* given by Wallace (*Malay Archipelago*, Vol. I., p. 212), shews the huge bill and prominent crest which Chinese artists at Canton transfer to the head of an otherwise graceful but purely imaginary crane. The ornaments carved at Canton from the wax-like substance of the crest are well known to residents in China.
† See Note V. at foot.

tablets of gold and one hundred tablets of silver. Of ingots of silver they carried forty thousand. Great, in sooth, were the cost and pains of this expedition; and yet, withal, it returned discomfited. Not so has it been in the days of our Sovereign the Exalted Founder, when, without need of a single warlike armament, for more than one hundred and fifty years tribute has been sent without misliking or remissness. Could such things come to pass with those who lie pillowed on the ocean far away, unless a Sovereign commissioned from on high were in our midst ? Would men be willing, were it otherwise, to fare submissively so far across the seas, and to confess allegiance within the limits of the Empire ?

NOTE I.—The notices of Java supplied by the Chinese historical compilations have been collected by Amiot in the *Mémoires concernant les Chinois*, tom. 14, and the originals may be referred to in the *Yüan Kien Lui Han* Cyclopædia, B. 234. It is here stated that Kwa Wa 瓜哇 is the same as the country anciently known by the name of Chê-p'o 闍婆. Another name for it is P'u-ka-lung 蒲家龍 (probably the modern Pekalongan). Amiot, following, it is charitable to presume, some Chinese authority, proceeds to explain that " Les Yuen ou les Mongoux sont les premiers qui lui aient donné le nom de *Koua-oua*, qui signifie *son de courge*, parce que le son de voix des peuples de ce Royaume approche beaucoup de celui que rend une courge sèche, quand ou la frappe, ou qu'on la fait rouler par terre !" It is a decided act of injustice to the memory of the Mongols to saddle them with this piece of eighteenth century etymology. The Mongols, or rather the Chinese who fought and wrote in their service, designated the island we know as Java quite correctly by means of the characters 爪哇 Chao-wa, as may be seen to this day in the Chronicle of the Yüan dynasty, compiled from the records they bequeathed. The addition of a single dash to the character *chao* converts it into *kwa*, and supplies P. Amiot with his vocal theory. The first mention of the island by a Chinese writer occurs in the *Fo-kwoh-ki* of Fah Hien, who, on his return voyage from India, after many perils and anxieties, arrived in the country of Yeh-p'o-t'i 耶婆堤. This was long ago identified by Landresse, in his annotations of Rémusat's work, with the Yava dwipa or "Island of Barley" which makes its appearance for the first time in Ptolemy's map, about the middle of the second century of our era. Fah Hien's voyage took place in about the year A. D. 413; and only a few years later direct intercourse between the Hindu sovereigns of Java and the Chinese court was inaugurated by the first of a long series of embassies. The Yü Hai 玉海 Cyclopædia, compiled in the 13th century by Wang Ying-lin, supplies the means of tracing these successive missions from their earliest date. In the section headed "Tributary Relations" 朝貢 (Books 152 to 151 of the work) it is stated that in the 9th and the 12th years of Yüan Kia of the earlier Sung dynasty (A.D. 432 and 435) "embassies arrived from the country of Ho-ling 訶陵, otherwise called She-wa 闍婆, which lies in the midst of the southern ocean, had cities walled with timber, possessed a written language, and was acquainted with the science of astronomy. At the summer solstice a staff eight *ch'ih* high was erected there, which cast a shadow to the south 2 *ch'ih* 4 *ts'un* in length." In the name Ho-ling, or Ko-ling, which is given here as appertaining to Java, one is tempted to recognize the Kalinga of the Coromandel coast, from which the earliest Hindu invaders of the island appear to have proceeded. (Cf. Crawfurd, *Hist. Ind. Archipel.*, II., p. 226). It is curious to note, in this connection, that in speaking of the trade between India and Java, which Crawfurd states "has always been chiefly conducted from the ports of Coromandel and by the nation called Kalinga or Telinga," he adds that "the Teliugas, more expert and

skiful navigators than the Chinese, have learned from the Arabs, who had their knowledge of the Greeks, to take the sun's altitude with the forestaff." (*Hist. Ind. Archipel.*, III., p. 197). The *Yüan Kien Lui Han* Cyclopædia (B. 231) gives under the head of "Java" a highly interesting document in the shape of the actual credentials presented by the envoys who visited the Chinese court in the reign above mentioned. Nothing could exceed the humility of tone with which, in this *piao* 表 or respectful Address, the sovereign of Shé-p'o-p'o-ta 闍婆婆達國, named She-li-p'o-ta-t'o-a-lo-pa-ma, is made to pour out his expressions of loyalty "at the feet of the great King of the land of Sung, the Great Fortunate One, the Son of Heaven." It is very noteworthy that the imagery of this document is conspicuously Buddhistic. The Chinese sovereign is addressed in a strain of fulsome adulation, as he whose kingdom is wide-spreading and his people many in number, whose palaces and cities are in the likeness of Heaven (忉利天宮, the heaven of Trayastrimsha), the title of which is Ta Sung, the great kingdom of Chow," and the sovereign himself is likened by implication to the possessor of all wisdom, the subjugator of the Màras, he who turned the wheel of the law, who brought salvation to all created beings, and who, this task completed, has entered upon Nirvâna, etc. etc. The compilers of the *Yüan Kien Lui Han* omit to name the source whence this document is derived; but if, as may fairly be assumed, it is a genuine extract from the records of the period, it serves to fix the date at which Buddhism had already found its way into Java. On the other hand, the scribes employed to draw up the document in Chinese may also, perhaps, be credited with having added flourishes of their own invention to the Javanese text. The address continues with a proffer of allegiance, inspired by the admiration which, even far beyond the seas, has been excited by the bounties diffused from the fountain of universal benevolence. If his offer be accepted, the King entreats that a message be sent to him in the same year. He commissions 佛大陀婆 Fuh-ta-t'o-p'o as his chief, and Koh-ti 葛抵 as his assistant envoy, requesting that a hearing and credence be given to what T'o-p'o has to unfold ; and he expresses his hope that the requests to be preferred may be acceded to. Some trifling presents, in token of the humble feelings cherished, are presented with this royal letter.

Notwithstanding these tenders of allegiance—and, perhaps, in consequence of a refusal to join in the projects indicated in the credentials which embody them—the Chinese records state that no further embassies arrived from Java until more than five hundred years later, in A.D. 992, the third year of the reign Ch'un Hwa of the Sung dynasty. The sovereign by whom this mission was despatched is said to have been named Muh-lo-ch'a 木羅茶. The Yü Hai records that his ambassadors landed at Ming Chow (the modern Ningpo), and arrived four months afterwards at the Court (then established at Pien Liang in Honan), with tribute of ivory-tusks, pearls, cowry shells, and white parrots. The next embassy arrived about A.D. 1110 ; and, after this, relations again became suspended for a century and a half, until the majesty of China was once more asserted in the hands of the Mongol invader. The expedition to Java undertaken by Kublai is discussed in Note III. below.

NOTE II.—The mention of Ts'üan Chow, commonly known at the present day as Chin-chew, one of the principal cities of Fuhkien, as the port at which the expedition against Java was embarked, invites some farther notice of this spot, more particularly in respect of its identification with the Zaiton or Caiton of Marco Polo's narrative. Since the days of Klaproth, no room for doubt has been left on this subject, and the recent labours of Pauthier and Yule have accumulated a mass of evidence confirmatory of

Polo's statements regarding this celebrated emporium. During the last year or two, however, Mr. G. Phillips has brought forward some interesting particulars in connection with the port anciently known as Geh-kong 月港, on the site of which the present city of Hai-ch'éng Hien 海澄縣, in the neighbourhood of Amoy, is built; and he has contended that Chang-chow, not Ts'üan Chow, was the Chinese emporium of the middle ages, which was described by Polo, Ibn Batuta, and other travellers, under the name of Zaiton. In the latest edition of his work, Colonel Yule has met, so far as was necessary, the contention raised in favour of Chang-chow, and whilst admitting, what is undeniably the fact, that in the 15th century Chang-chow had become the resort of travellers, merchants, and missionaries from foreign countries, he points to the fact that Ts'üan Chow, and Ts'üan Chow almost alone, is the port of debarkation mentioned in historical notices of the arrival of ships and missions from abroad during the reign of Kublai, and of departure for his foreign expeditions. (*The Book of Marco Polo*, London, 1875, Vol. II., p. 221). In elucidation of the ancient importance of Ts'üan Chow as a commercial emporium, some extracts from Chinese sources, in addition to those amassed by Pauthier, may be given here. In the great Imperial Geography compiled by order of the Emperor K'ien Lung, entitled 大清一統志, or Description of the Empire, historical as well as topographical details are comprised in the account given of each prefecture. Under the head of Ts'üan-chow Fu, we read the following of Chén Téh-siu, who governed this city under the Sung dynasty. "When Chen Téh-siu was governor in the reign of Ning Tsung (A.D. 1195-1224), the foreign shipping stood in such dread of the oppressive taxes then levied that not more than three or four vessels came in the course of a year. Chén Téh-siu took the lead in affording them relief, upon which the numbers rapidly increased to as many as 36." A century earlier than this, Tu Ch'un held the office of Judge at Ts'üan Chow, and of him it is related that "in his time the place was largely frequented by foreign shipping 湴船, and merchandize of all descriptions was piled up there mountain-high. The officials of the city were used to trade privily on their own account, paying not so much as one-tenth of the value of what they bought. The only persons who did not engage themselves in this illicit traffic were the Governor, whose name was Kwan Yung, and Tu Ch'un. Nothing was known for a time of the conduct that was practised, but it eventually came to light and was brought before the tribunals. Tu Ch'un and Kwan Yung alone escaped the punishment that ensued." In the same section, the following description is given of what must have been the principal anchorage of the port of Ts'üan Chow.· "An-hai Ch'ông 安海城 lies 60 *li* south-east from Tsin-kiang 晉江 (the district seat of government within the walls of Ts'üan Chow). It was anciently called Wan Hai. Early in the Sung dynasty (*i.e.* about the last quarter of the 10th century) it received the name of An-hai She 安海市 (trading-place of An-hai). The eastern side is called the old town, and the western the new town. When sea-going ships arrived, the officials at the city (*i.e.* Ts'üan Chow) sent an officer to collect duties at this place. The name Shih-tsing Tsin 石井津 was [also] given to the place; and in the fourth year of Kien Yen (A.D. 1130) a military command was established here under the name Shih-tsing Chên 石井鎭. A rampart of earth was thrown up in the 26th year of the reign Shao Hing (A.D. 1156) when the place was beleaguered by sea-rovers. Under the Yüan dynasty a deputy-Magistrate was established here with the title of supervisor of Shih-tsing; but in the 20th year of Hung Wu (A.D. 1397) the deputy-Magistrate was removed to Ch'ên-k'ang Chên 陳坑鎭 in the T'ung-an district, upon which the place again became a great

resort for traders." The collectorate of Customs 税務司 for the port of Ts'üan Chow under the Yüan dynasty is elsewhere stated to have been fixed at a point called T'ang She 塘市, 20 *li* South of Tsin-kiang.

Mr. Phillips has doubted whether the seat of government of the Viceroyalty of Fuh-kien was established at Fuhchow at the time of Marco Polo's visit; but the precision of the Chinese historical records leaves no room for doubt in this respect. The *Yh T'ung Che* states that in the 15th year of the reign Che Yüan (A.D. 1278), *i.e.* at the moment of the final collapse of the expiring Sung dynasty, a Viceroyalty 行中書省 was established at Ts'üan Chow, but that in A.D. 1281 the seat of government was removed to Fuh Chow. In the year following the seat of government was moved back to Ts'üan Chow, but in the next year after that it again returned to Fuh Chow. (大清一統志, B. 260-264).

With reference to the importance of Ts'üan Chow under the Yüan dynasty as an emporium of the shipping trade of the Indian and eastern seas, authorities by the dozen might be adduced from the records of that period; but the following interesting passage from the chronicle of the reign of Kublai will suffice to shew that this port, not Chang Chow, was the principal mart of Fuhkien at the period now in question. In the 30th year of the reign Che Yüan (A.D. 1293), it is recorded, "assent was given to the proposal made by Liu Mêng-yen, that Superintendents of Trade and Shipping 市船司 should be appointed at Hang Chow, Shang-hai, Kan-p'u, Wên Chow, K'ing-yüan (the modern Ningpo), Kwangtung (Canton), and Ts'üan Chow; and that as an assessment of three in thirty was levied on merchandize at Ts'üan Chow, whilst elsewhere the rate was only one in fifteen, the practice prevailing at Ts'üan Chow should be adopted as the general rule" (元史, B. 17). It is evident, moreover, from the statements handed down respecting the expeditions of Chêng Ho and his colleagues, that so late as toward the middle of the fifteenth century the port still retained its character as a place of embarkation for foreign voyages.

A geographical detail which is noted in the *Ta Ts'ing Yih T'ung Che* appears to throw some light on a doubtful passage in Marco Polo's account of Fuhchow, beside tending to elucidate the manner in which foreign trade was carried on in the immediate neighbourhood of that port at the time to which his narrative refers. In the text followed by Pauthier we read *(Livre de M. Polo*, cap. clv., p. 527): "Pres de cette cité est li ports de Kayteu, qui entre en la mer occeanne. Et va ledit fleuve à ce port. Ilz ont moult beaux jardins et désirables. Et si est moult belle cité et bien ordonnée." For Pauthier's *Kayteu* both Marsden and Yule read Zaiton, which may, indeed, be not improbably the correct rendering (Kayton being a very likely error of transcription for Çaiton); and Pauthier's proposal to fabricate a Chinese name of *Hai-théou* 海 頭, as a possible equivalent of *Ma-théou* or "landing-place," in order to provide an identification for *Kayteu*, is only too characteristic of his facile imagination. A port called 海 口 Hai K'ow (Sea-Port), did indeed flourish at the mouth of the Min during the Ming dynasty; and it is singular that this fact should have been overlooked by Pauthier in his anxiety to find a local habitation for Polo's "belle cité;" but the point to which attention is now to be directed is still another. In the Topography of the Empire, already quoted from above, the following description is given of the Hai-t'an group of islands, lying some thirty miles south of the entrance to the river Min: " The Hai-t'an islands 海 壇 山 lie 120 *li* eastward from the district of Ch'ang-loh, in the midst of the sea. They are 300 *li* in circuit. Under the T'ang dynasty they were employed as a pasturage for horses. The Sung dynasty appointed an official to superintend the pasturage, which appoint-

ment was subsequently abolished. In the reign Hwang-Yeo (A.D. 1048-1054) the people were allowed to bring the land under tillage. In the reign Shun Hi (A.D. 1174-1189) three thousand and odd families were settled here. Under the Yüan dynasty the number of families reached the amount of forty thousand, principally engaged in the fishery. In the 20th year of Hung Wu (A.D. 1387) a decree commanded the population to be removed to the mainland. Upon this the territory was laid waste." After a number of topographical details of the various channels and anchorages, the account is concluded with the statement that " this was a great place of resort for shipping 舶 船 之 都 會. Subsequently to the period of the Five Dynasties (which terminated *circa* A. D. 960) it became a mart where the seafaring traders dealt with each other 海 賈 互 市 之 地; and it was commonly called ' Little Yang Chow 小 楊 州 ' (Yang Chow being a city exceptionally famous for its wealth and luxury). In the early years of the Ming dynasty the population was removed to the mainland." It seems at least not impossible that this may be the port described by Marco Polo in the following terms, as given by Colonel Yule (Vol. II., 2nd ed., p. 216); " *Il hi se fait grand mercandies de perles e d'autres pieres presiose, e ce est porce que les nés de Yndie hi viennent con maint merchaant qe usent en les ysles de Endie ; et encore voz di que ceste ville est près au port de Caiton en la mer Osiane ; et illuec vienent maintes nés de Indie con maintes mercandies, e puis cest part vienent les nés por le grant flum jusque à la cité de Fugui.*"

The Hai-t'an Islands are in the district of Ch'ang-loh ; and it was at a port in this district that the great naval expedition of 1431 made its first stoppage on the coast before proceeding on its voyage to the South (See *ante*, Part II., Note II.)

NOTE III.—Beyond fragmentary allusions such as those in the text, no account of the great expedition fitted out by Kublai against Java is to be found elsewhere than in the

Chronicle of the Yüan dynasty. In the history of Kublai's reign itself, the notices of this undertaking are, as usual, extremely brief. Under the 29th year of the portion of his reign styled Che Yüan, or A.D. 1292, it is recorded that "the T'ai K'ing 太卿 of Ts'üan Chow, Ihamish 亦黑迷失, the 'commander of ten thousand,' She Pih 史弼, and the vice-Governor of Fuhkien, Kao Hing 高興, were named in the second moon joint High Counsellors of the vice-Royalty of Fuhkien, and placed in command of the expedition against Java. Five hundred vessels, large and small, and twenty thousand troops were employed for this purpose." In the seventh moon it is recorded that the three commanders were summoned into the imperial presence, and it is further added that his Majesty, in personally addressing the departing generals, gave special charge of all arrangements concerning the fleet to Ihamish, as one experienced in navigation, and the chief command of the land forces to Kao-Hing. The only additional mention of the expedition occurs under the twelfth moon of the 30th year, which corresponds (as we should now reckon) with January, 1294, only a month before Kublai's death, where it is recorded that "for their want of success, Ihamish, She Pih, Kao Hing, and their associates, on their return, were punished with blows, disgraced, and mulcted in one-third of their household goods." The details which are omitted in these laconic notices are supplied in the biographies of the three commanders themselves, forming part of the section of the Yüan Chronicle devoted to individual histories, and in the account of their expedition furnished under the head of Java in Book 97. Of Ihamish we learn (列傳, B. 18,) that he was a Uigur by birth, who, from employment in the imperial guards, was selected by Kublai early in his reign for the office of envoy to foreign countries. In A.D. 1264, on returning from a mission to Champa, he was despatched to Ceylon to obtain a sight of the Holy Grail of Buddhism, the relic of the pàtra or almsbowl of Shákyamuni. A few years later he was sent on a mission to Malabar. His many voyages marked him out for service when the expedition to Java was contemplated. She Pih, the generalissimo of the landforces, (B. 19,) was a highly distinguished soldier and was acting as Governor of Cheh-kiang at the time of his appointment to this post. Kao Hing, his lieutenant, was another of the trusted generals of Kub-lai, who bestowed numerous gifts of value upon him at the time of his appointment. It is in his biography that we meet with the cause assigned for the invasion of Java. An envoy named Mèng K'i 孟琪, it appears, had been sent by Kublai to the island, and had returned, branded in the face by order of the native sovereign. It was to avenge this insult that the expedition was resolved upon. The provinces of Fuhkien, Kiangsi, and Hukwang furnished twenty thousand troops, who were equipped with provisions for a year, and with paper money to the value of four hundred thousand ounces of silver. Sailing from Ts'üan Chow in the beginning of A.D. 1293, when "owing to the rolling of the vessels in the stormy weather, the whole force was for several days unable to take food," they reached a halting point at Kow Lan, near the Carimata Islands, where a council of war was held 議方畧. In the 2nd moon Ihamish, with ten vessels and a force of five hundred men, went forward to summon the islanders to submission; and the main body of the force shortly afterwards followed him, and effected a landing on the shores of the 八節澗 or Strait of Madura. At this period, it is narrated, the kingdom of Chao-wa—which had its seat of government at Modjopahit—was at enmity with the neighbouring kingdom of Koh-lang 葛郎; and the King of Chao-wa, named 哈只葛達那加刺 Ha-chi-ko-ta-na-ka-la, had been slain by 哈只葛當 Ha-chi-ko-tang, King of Koh-lang. The son-in-law of the deceased sovereign, named 土罕必闍耶, T'u-han-pi-shé-yeh, had attacked the conqueror, but had been driven back to his defences at Modjopahit 麻喏八歇. On the arrival of the Chinese army he invoked its assistance, and joined his forces with those of· She Pih, who agreed to advance with him against Ta-ho 荅合,* the capital of the State of Koh-lang. The military measures taken in this campaign are circumstantially described, and it is stated that the army of Koh-lang, upwards of one hundred thousand strong, was defeated, whereupon Ha-ehi-koh-tang surrendered himself a prisoner, with his family and his ministers. T'u-han-pi-shé-yeh made entreaty for their release, on a formal attestation of submission being delivered, together with much store of precious stones and other valuables, to the Chinese commanders; and his request was granted. Meanwhile T'u-han-pi-shé-yeh's son, 昔刺八的昔剌丹 Si-la-pa-ti-si-la-tan, had revolted against the Chinese, and Kao Hing vainly sought to impress his colleagues with the dread of meditated treachery which he himself entertained. A guard of 200 men was sent as escort with T'u-han-pi-shé-yeh on his return to his capital (or, as one account alleges, with the King of Koh-lang), and this party was set upon and massacred by the perfidious T'u-han-pi-shé-yeh. The mask being thus thrown off, he attacked the Chinese army as it was retiring to the coast, taking it at a disadvantage in a narrow defile. She Pih himself commanded the rear, and by maintaining a running fight for a distance of 300 li (one hundred miles) he succeeded in reaching his ships. This was about three months after the landing had been effected. The armament having been reëmbarked, it was conducted back

* This, it seems highly probable, was Doho, mentioned by Crawford as one of the principal native states of Java during the centuries preceding the introduction of Muhommedanism. The ruins of Doho, he states, " are in the fertile district of Kadiri, about the centre of the island, counting by its length, and toward the southern coast." (*Hist. Ind. Archipel.*, II., p. 299).

to Ts'üan Chow by a voyage of sixty-eight days' duration. The loss incurred was upwards of three thousand men. On the landing of the force, an inventory was taken by the officers of government of the treasures that were brought back with it, consisting in gold, gems, scented woods, cotton cloths, and other booty, the value of which was estimated at more than 500,000 ounces of silver. During the absence of the main body of the force, moreover, commissioners had been sent to conciliate the allegiance of the lesser states, and She Pih was able to produce a respectful letter, engrossed on a golden scroll, from the King of Muh-li 没里 (Bali?), with presents of gold and silver, ivory, rhinoceros horns, etc. For the miscarriage of the expedition, notwithstanding, Kublai condemned She Pih to the penalty of 17 blows, and to confiscation of one-third of his property. In the following year, however, on the accession of a new sovereign, he was restored to favour and created a Minister of State.

NOTE IV.—The statement respecting the Javanese era is derived from the *Sing Ch'a*, in which it is alleged that " at the end of official letters in this country, they write the date 1376. On examination, the epoch is found to commence in the period of the Han dynasty, coming down to the seventh year of the reign Süan Têh of our dynasty of Ta Ming." The 7th year of Süan Têh corresponds with A.D. 1432, in which year, as we have already seen, a great Chinese expedition visited Java, and the commencement of the Javanese era should be placed, accordingly, in A.D. 57. There is a difference of some 20 years, however, for which it is not easy to account, between this date and the period assigned by Crawfurd as that with which the Javanese chronology begins. He states that " an examination of the institutions of the Indian islanders furnishes an argument, and, as far as I know, one only, in favour of the hypothesis of *Kalinga* being the native country of those who propagated Hinduism in the Indian islands. This argument is drawn from a comparison of the kalenders of Southern India, and that which prevailed in the Indian islands. The year in Karnata and Telinga is lunar, with an interealary month in every thirty, and the era commences with the birth of *Salivana* or *Saka*, 78 years after Christ. This, with all its particulars, is the kalender which prevailed in Java, and which at present obtains in the Hindu country of Bali, as its name, *Saka warsa chandra*, distinctly implies." (*Hist. Ind. Archipel.*, II., p. 229.) Sir Stamford Raffles, in his *History of Java*, seems to admit a further variation of three years, when he writes that "the Hindu empire of Majapàhit was overthrown in the first year of the 15th century of the Javan era, or about the year of our Lord 1475," (Vol. II., p. 66). In the absence of material for a fuller investigation, this question can only be left as it stands.

NOTE V.—The majority of the names occurring in this long catalogue of foreign products are the same with those in common use at the present day, as identified by Williams in his *Chinese Commercial Guide*, and more fully by Dr. F. P. Smith in his *Chinese Materia Medica*. To this work in particular obligation must be expressed for the identification of the drug *wu-tieh-ni* 烏爹泥 with catechu, or, as it was formerly designated by pharmaceutists, *terra japonica*, the brownish cakes in which the drug is seen suggesting to both Europeans and Chinese the idea of an earth (*ni*). Its common name in China at the present day is *urh ch'a* 兒茶. For the "native red earth" 番紅土 of the text no positive identification can be suggested. The "rose-dew" or rose water (? attar) 薔薇露, appears to have been more familiarly known to the Chinese of the middle ages than in later times. It is mentioned in the Treatise on Perfumes 香譜, a work which according to K'ien Lung's Bibliography (四庫全書目錄) dates from the Sung dynasty, under the name of *tsiang-wei shuei*, or, literally, rose-water, and is defined as a scent ("dew") distilled from flowers in the

country of the Persians 大食國. As a substitute for it in the present day (that is to say, about the 12th century of our era) the essence of the *mo-li* or jasmine flower is, it is said, employed. In A.D. 958, it is further added, fifteen flasks of the perfume were sent as a present to the Chinese Court from the kingdom of Kw'ĕn-ming 昆明, in the modern region of Yünnan, with the statement that it had been obtained from *Si Yü* — Central Asia. Clothing imbued with the scent, it is observed in conclusion, may decay sooner than the perfume disappear (*Kĕh Che King Yüan*, B. 57).

The *ma t'ĕng hiang* 蔴籐香, literally *ma* (or "hemp") rattan gum or resin, may not improbably be gambodge, which is commonly known as *t'ĕng hwang*, or "rattan yellow." The *t'ĕng kieh* 籐竭 is another drug which must be left unidentified. It may be imagined to be somewhat akin to the "dragon's blood," 血竭, a resinous substance, blood-red in colour, which is believed to be the product of *Pterocarpus draco*. The *ma pieh tsze* of China are the seeds of *muricia cochinchinese*, a cucurbitaceous plant, which grows wild in the southern provinces. The Javanese drug to which the same name is given in the text may be the product of another but similar species. The drug named *lu hwei*, commonly named by Europeans "aloes," is in reality, according to Dr. Bretschneider, (*Arabs and Arabian Colonies etc.*, p. 20), brown catechu. The "vermin destroying preparation," "pottery stone" 碗石, and *wu hiang* (black gum or resin) of the text are unidentified. For particulars relating to the drugs that are named, see Smith's *Chinese Materia Medica*. The kingfisher-feathers 翠毛 are, doubtless, the plumage, of exquisite blue-green tints, used at the present day in the manufacture of enamelled ornaments, principally for female headgear, in all parts of China. The precise nature of the *mi* 蕊 cloth mentioned in the text—most probably some description of calico—must be left undetermined.

W. F. MAYERS.

AN INTRODUCTION TO A RETROSPECT OF FORTY YEARS OF FOREIGN INTERCOURSE WITH CHINA,

AND

A REVIEW OF HER RELATIONS WITH JAPAN.*

A retrospect of the past four decades of Foreign intercourse with China, presents two strikingly dissimilar pictures to the present observer. One that of the regime of monopoly in trade to the exclusion of all political and social relations. The other, the establishment of relations of comity and a progressive amelioration of intercourse generally.

Yet it is, perhaps, only to one who like myself has spent the most of the forty years here that the contrasts of the two periods are distinctly marked. And certainly none other than an old resident and close observer could adequately measure the gain from this amelioration of intercourse during the past fifteen years;—gain especially in the solidifying elements of government. It is necessary to have felt the utter instability of affairs in the period of 1848 to 1858 especially and to have witnessed the visible progress of the past ten years, to appreciate the change.

Without presuming to apportion the blame that attaches undeniably to foreign contact as well as to domestic misrule, especially during the demoralized reign of the present Emperor's father, I have no hesitation in declaring that the renovation of China, like that of Turkey and Japan, is from without.

* A lecture delivered at Concordia Hall, Canton, December 8th, 1874.

This is speaking in the broader sense and irrespective of the accidents of the time however produced; such as the critical position of the Dynasty and its support by Foreigners: and it is also in recognition of the natural and moral law, that Nations—like individuals —must work out their own destinies.

We naturally first regard Nations in their relations with our own and other countries, as the first step is to gain access to them; the second, to study their domestic polity and social traits.

A traveller, — for his perfect enjoyment and satisfaction, as well as from a sense of right,— should visit Foreign countries in the same frame of mind as that in which Professor Heeren tells us he entered upon the study of different Nations: namely: " by making it a fixed rule, to banish as much as possible from his mind every preconceived conjecture and hypothesis, and to describe every Nation as he actually found it: And that his notion of States was such that he never could consider them as mere machines, but always regarded them in the light of moral personages, each having its own manner of living, moving, and acting ; and the elucidation of this is, in his opinion, alone worthy to be called statistics, and not the compilation of barren tables, containing figures instead of things."

It is in this philosophical spirit and with a

similar broad scope of vision that I invite my audience to regard the Empire of China. The subject is vast and complicated, and we are but at the threshold, whether of time or place. It comprises many peoples, speaking differing tongues, ruled by an alien Dynasty: and a history whose authentic annals extend more than three thousand years.

We may note some indications of the past; but we cannot apply them with unerring prophecy to the future.

I speak from personal observation, and my primary purpose is to present the prominent events of the past forty years as marking the salient points of Foreign intercourse; whilst illustrating a general narrative by personal reminiscences of social life, which serve to shew changes coincident with political progress and to animate pages else of dry seeming to readers other than students of history. From my habit of preparing reports periodically to send abroad, I am enabled to verify my narrative; and as I recorded events irrespective of their direct bearing upon Foreign relations, my work as a whole should be more comprehensively historical of the immediate period than any of those treating of preceding periods have been, and present somewhat more than an outline of the recent history of China. But as to a general survey of the Empire,—its previous history, its geography, its general aspect and resources, and the manners and customs of its peoples—the works of Sir John Davis and Dr. Wells Williams, entitled respectively,—"A general description of the Empire of China;" and "The Middle Kingdom," left little to be desired (by the general reader at least,) down to the period of their publication, about thirty years ago. My purpose, therefore, in the course of lectures, to which this is introductory, is simply to continue a narrative, to which I was originally invited here, in a form to aid future historians, whilst presently acceptable to the general public.

In regarding China according to the dictum of Heeren, as already quoted, i.e. in the light of an assemblage of moral personages, we must keep in view the qualifying circumstance that the people subject to the Emperor's sway are not homogeneous in the strict sense that the historian intended, in thus speaking of States in general. They are not so, owing to the diversities in race, in dialect, and in the customs and conditions of society, such as the element of clanism, for instance; all serving more or less to localise opinion, feeling and action and to neutralise the spirit of nationality.

In the absence of the compact elements of national life, presenting tangible evidences of vitality as a general body-politic, we must regard the diversities which constitute them, rather as neighboring friendly communities allied for common purposes, than one homogeneous people. And as subjects of one Empire, we must view them as politically divided into two classes, the governing class and the governed; the former composed of the Literati, the latter of the "Min" or the people in general; but with the qualifying reconciling compensation to the subject class, that its members are all eligible to compete for the honors and emoluments of the literary and governing body. And hereat we recognize the most powerful and conservative bond existing between the Emperor and people, which superadded to the sentimental one of filial piety, has held the majority to their allegiance amidst internal and external counteractions of the most threatening character; and which alone beget confidence in the future, in presence of obvious elements of demoralization in a system of government whose parts are constantly presenting the appearance of dislocation.

To adequately estimate and comprehend the Chinese as a people distinct from the ruling alien Dynasty, we must judge them by their Literature rather than by their general polity. Their external force is traditionally, if it has not always been feeble; but by their literature they conquer their military conquerors, as the Roman tongue reconquered the Goths and Northmen who overran that Empire.

Were they a more homogeneous people reared in the use of but one vernacular dialect, their cohesion and hence their external power had long since made them the most formidable of Nations. Their force as a people is lost in lack of the concentration of thought and expression that leads to common apprehension and conception and thence to united action. And thence is derived the obviously-cherished policy of their Rulers, to abstain from healing the animosities of different races and clans, and aid, rather, in perpetuating the diversities which exist.

While such diversities and animosities characterize the masses of the people, the Literati,—elevated into a distinct class and forming the higher mind of the Nation, bound to the Dynasty by the system of education and preferment to office,—is groping in abstruse or purposeless disquisition or dreamy pedantry, in the classical dialect. And the state of the Empire in this respect may be likened to that of the countries of Western and Southern Europe when, after being overrun by the Goths and Northmen, they retained the Latin language and were, in turn, reconquered by the power it conferred on the Priesthood; when Ecclesiastical Rome became more widely dominant than military Rome had been, and all who were ambitious of advancement cultivated her language. This eventually led to a state of mental bondage or stagnation which, as described by a learned author, reminds one, at most points, of the tendencies so obvious among the Literati of China and the consequent influences upon its national life; while it suggests considerations of the possibilities of the future analogous to the changes wrought in Europe by a cultivation of its vernacular languages.

The learned author alluded to says:—
"This was the useful age of critical erudition. It furnished the studious with honors and avocations; but they were reserved only for themselves. They transcribed as sacred what authority had long established. . . . This state was a heritage of ideas and of opinions, transmitted from age to age with little addition or diminution: Authority and quotation closed all arguments and filled vast volumes; and a week of agony was exhausted on a page finely inlaid with a mosaic of phrases: All native vigor died away in the coldness of imitation; and a similarity of thinking and of style deprived the writers of that raciness which the nations of Europe subsequently displayed when they cultivated their vernacular literature."

Such was the picture of the stunted intellectual life of the countries of western and southern Europe drawn by the erudite author; and I venture to think that it presents a remarkable parallel of the mental life of China at this day.

And a fresh illustration of the all-but-idolatrous pedantry of the Literati, in connection with the written language, may be seen in the placing of receptacles for loose scraps of it found in the street, all over the city and neighbouring towns, with placarded injunctions to rescue all such from the desecration of being trampled upon, which is a trait analogous to the deification of speech in the early ages of mankind, and akin also to that of the devotees of Mohammed, to which the lamented Charles Dickens alludes in the following Stanzas.

"They have a superstition in the East,
    That Allah, written on a piece of paper,
Is better unction than can come of Priest,
    Of rolling incense, and of lighted taper;
Holding that any scrap which bears that name,
In any character its front impressed on,
Shall help the finder through the burning flame,
    And give his toasted feet a place to rest on."

Pursuing our inquiries into the causes of the renovation of thought in Europe, we find that until, by the cultivation of the vernacular dialects, the period arrived when the masses of the several peoples could be effectively appealed to, each in their own vernacular, the trammels of Rome were not relaxed; and, indeed, that the exclusive scholastic adherence to the Latin language continued to fetter the general mind of the West until the Reformation.[*]

There is not the same indissoluble and exclusive connection between Confucianism and the written language of China as there was between Roman Catholicism and the Latin language;[†] but even on this point the parallel holds true. The secret memorial of Tseng-quo-fan to the Emperor in 1868, in reply to a confidential note of the Tsungle Yamen, claims for Confucianism, however, in contradistinction to the Religions of the West, that it has stood the test of time, while they are inconstant; his words being, " It is very evident that the different Religions fluctuate from time to time in their vigor. On the other hand Confucianism has not suffered attrition through myriads of ages and it has regenerated China in government, morals, manners and doctrines. It was somewhat obscured after the Ts'in and Han dynasties, while Buddhism had its rise in India, and it is now supplanted in a great measure by Mohammedanism there. Roman-Catholicism arose in the East and West. Now Protestantism has sprung up in the East and West, and opposes Roman Catholicism with much power." This was a part of the reply of this great Mandarin, when Viceroy at Nanking, at the period of the proposed revision of the Treaties; and it is somewhat ingenious as a plea for Confucianism.

Confucianism exacts, of course, the outward homage of the Literati. China has, however, been a land of comparative tolerance as respects Religious ideas pure and simple; she has been jealous only of political intrigue and doctrines subversive of order.

* " That deluge called the Reformation," as Archbishop Manning phrases it.
† For Confucianism " is in practical life quite alloyed with Shamanistic and Buddhistic ideas and practices," as Faber says.

And it has been by precept and injunction, rather than persecution, that the Confucian doctrines have been propagated. The Religion of the Tartars was Buddhism, but they yielded the preëminence to Confucianism, and thus pay homage directly to the higher civilization of the Chinese whom they conquered. Politically the watchword of the Tartars was "divide and conquer," and it still holds good, as we see, in their policy. Just as the hostile relations of the different factions in ancient Britain subserved the purposes of the Roman conquerors, so the hostility of clans and segregated communities in China, is welcome to the Manchu Dynasty. And whether, if their conquerors left them, as the Romans did our ancestors after 400 years of rule, the Chinese would lapse into discord again, as our ancestors did, is a very interesting subject of conjecture.

But the pregnant question of the day is :— Will the regeneration of the Chinese people be attained by the tentative course of policy which comprises the bolstering-up of the ' sick man' at Peking for an indefinite period, a course fraught with general incertitude and some positive perils, but admitting of a gradual infusion of Western ideas that may eventuate in a national renovation of thought ?

If this method is the most commendable, an attempt to assimilate the differing dialects, which seems to be desiderated by a learned student of Chinese (Rev. John Chalmers) would be a useful step; since this implies a policy of conciliation, in lieu of antagonism. Obviously united action cannot be predicated of the present condition of the people in relation to each other in respect to diversities of dialects, customs, clan animosities and differing incentives to discontent or loyalty.

Nothing short of the revival of some ancient tyranny affecting a large majority of the people, will, under circumstances like the present, lead them to act so far in concert as to break the continuity of the chain that holds them to the routine of the ancients,—a routine that their alien Rulers, with so much astuteness, sedulously pursues.

A distinguished historian, writing of the reign of the Emperor Charles the 5th, says: "durability is not the test of merit in human institutions. Tried by the only touchstone applicable to Government, their capacity to insure the highest welfare of the governed, we shall not find his polity deserving of much admiration."

I think this dictum requires qualification, and that durability is a test though not the sole test, because it must always imply in some degree the actual welfare of the people; and China is an example of general prosperity under a polity of unprecedented durability. Nor have there been wanting experimental tests of great severity, irrespective of external influences, to confirm the people in a reliance upon its fundamental principles. For, in fact, China's national life has been threatened from within as well as without and subject to great vicissitudes and ample experience. And it is curious to observe that the experiment of the Paris Commune three years ago, upon a small scale,—as it was in effect,—was but a repetition of what occurred in China 800 years ago, when it was extended to the whole Empire during a portion of two Reigns. But the people soon saw the disintegrating tendency of an imposed socialism that practically discouraged industry and individual effort; and after several struggles between the respective partisans, the socialists were finally banished the country. An incident of great historical interest in itself, as they united themselves to the cause of Genghis Khan and aided the conquest of their own country.

The system of the socialists was in fact reactionary, since it wholly deprived the people of individual initiative and responsibility, and hence of self-reliance and of all incentive to industry; and, therefore, intensified instead of mitigating the evil tendencies of the ancient routine.

As to sudden change, we are admonished against precipitancy by some memorable utterances of Dr. Dollinger and the other "old Catholics," who in their reply to the invitation of the Evangelical Alliance at New York last autumn, wrote as follows:— "Great changes will be necessary to attain the end in view. It can only be reached by reflection and a wise choice of ways and means. Therefore we were not disconcerted at the irony of those who said 'you only reject the infallibility of the Pope; you wish to retain all the other absurdities.' We have overcome the desire existed among ourselves for a sudden change, since we have all come to the belief that the prejudices and ideas in which successive generations have been educated cannot be destroyed in a single night. It has become manifest to all of us that our reform will be far more efficient if we proceed with deliberation, because experience will then teach us to detect in the good we introduce the shadow of evil."

There is wisdom in this matured conclusion, no doubt; and we may apply it to China so far as to acknowledge that her Rulers would do well to heed 'a shadow of evil' that we can at once discern in a too radical change affecting the fundamental principle of filial piety; which, so far as it does not partake of superstition or reach absolute submission, may be regarded as the most commendable feature of the Chinese polity.

We may recall a memorable instance of filial affection in the erection of the magnificent Pocelain Pagoda at Nanking, by an Emperor to the memory of his Mother, which was destroyed during the Taeping rebellion. And an anecdote of another dutiful son furnishes a happy illustration of this virtue: who, when a full grown man, submitting himself to the customary chastisement of his old mother, was rallied by a friend for weeping under the infliction of the bamboo, who said "surely she does not hurt you." "No alas!" sobbed the dutiful son, "my poor mother's strength lessens every day!" And an interesting instance in point that has occurred since this lecture was written is that of a son, whose father was compromised in the Che Me case at Chefoo and sentenced to receive 100 strokes of the Bamboo, beging to be allowed to suffer the punishment instead of his father; which the Magistrate, with the concurrence of the American Consul, who was also a member of the Court, permitted.

This feature is very pleasing in such examples; but, alas! there is a reverse picture of hideous aspect that makes one's heart's blood run cold and invokes the beneficent spirit that intoned the command " suffer little children to come unto me and forbid them not." The cruelty of parents to their children and husbands to their wives often presents a revolting picture; of which the law in China takes no cognizance or, rather, to which it accords immunity and even the praise of its administrators. A horrid instance of such is that of an unnatural father, a Mandarin of the high rank of Censor, who should himself be a pattern of virtue, as he no doubt was according to the code of his class, but who committed a deed that should for ever brand his name with the execration of mankind. It was Chun-tu-lau-yeh, who about 25 years ago had his daughter of 21 years of age immured in a tomb, built around her in the family cemetery a short distance from Peking: Her offence being an elopement with a man below her station, he being simply banished. Thus she was buried alive and left to die; and her terribly cruel fate has inspired the muse of a gifted writer * of Shanghai, who is also a student of the language; and has with much poetical skill endowed the high-born victim with the pathos of despair, as her own tongue reveals at once the piteous story of her doom and the tenacious love of life that God has implanted in the human heart.

Oh, what a fearful dream! Thank God I woke!
I thought I was within a noisome tomb immured,

* Mr. Stent.

Where all was dark; no sound the silence broke—
Ah, who can tell the terrors I endured!

Too horror-struck to even form a prayer,
I could but writhe upon the ground and scream;
Curse my hard fate, give way to wild despair,
And, wake at length—to find it all a dream.

I'll call my maid and bid her strike a light,
For even now I feel oppressed with fear;
How cold I am—I'll sleep no more to-night;
I shall feel better when the girl is here.

She does not come! Wherefore this awful gloom?
Why does my heart thus beat with unknown dread?
How came I hither? This is not my room,
It seems but little larger than my bed.

This is not my couch—'tis clammy ground!
Above my head a roof of stone I feel—
Stone, too, on either side—stone all around!
It *is* a tomb! Great God! my dream is *real!*

Help! save me! Let me not die like this—
A living death! Will no one heed my cries?
I stagger up, and reach an orifice,
To which I glue my hot and blood-shot eyes.

I never knew how beautiful it was till now
To watch the rising sun his radiance throw
O'er hill and dale, on every bush and bough—
Tinging all nature with a golden glow.

Help! Hither! save me! come and set me free!
My piercing screams attract the passers-by:—
Oh! are you men? Can you look on and see
A girl—a woman—shut up thus to die?

'Tis not the dread of death my heart appalls;
It is this lingering living death I fear,—
Shut up alive, to die within these walls,
Where every moment lengthens to a year.

Break down these walls! what if my crime
was great,
Say, could it merit such a death as this!
Kill me at once—if death *must* be my fate;
The hand that strikes the welcome blow,
I'll kiss!

Help, I implore you! 'Tis a woman calls!
I'm young and fair! Oh, save me from
this death!
Oh, snatch me from this tomb, break down
these walls,
And I will bless you with my latest
breath!

Help! Give me but my liberty—my life!
Save me from death—from this my living
grave!
Whoever saves me, I will be his wife—
His mistress—leman—minion—menial—
slave!

Poor though he be, his poverty I'll share:
The whole devotion of a life I'll give!
I'll toil for him—his troubles I will bear—
I'll beg for him—so he but bids me live.

Help! I am stifling! Oh! for the fresh pure
air!
To feel it on my hot and fevered cheeks!
Help! save me! or my very hands shall tear
These cursed walls! I'll rend them with
my shrieks!

Water! one drop, to quench my maddening
thirst!
My tongue is swollen—my throat is parched and dry!
Can this be death?—Father, you've done
your worst,
But oh! 'twas hard to doom me thus to
die!

The need of the warmth of Christianity to melt the stone-cold hearts of the stolid slaves of prescription, like the unnatural father of this hapless victim, could hardly be more eloquently enforced than by this spontaneous and affecting poem.

But as to the ways and means of change, I assume that the appeal of no Foreign Power would be answered by the people,—that, on the contrary, the greater the pressure from without the more adhesive will be Rulers and people; and that, hence, the alternative of the tentative process that is inseparable from a regime of nerveless grasp and irresolute jealousy, is the advent of some gifted and virtuous son of the soil, who, impatient of a sterile routine, shall summon his countrymen to a revolutionary change; or, better inspired, shall initiate a moral reformation more surely conserving the welfare of the people. The inspiration to this must be looked for, no doubt, from without; but our impatience may well be chastened by recalling the one fact, especially as it cannot have been forgotten by the Chinese, that but for our military and moral aid to the Manchu Government the Taeping Rebellion would have succeeded in achieving the independence of the middle and southern Provinces, at least: and thus have initiated a change analogous to that we see in Japan; rather in kind than degree, perhaps, yet similar as somewhat approximative of the customs of the West,—for it is not a little by the timid fear of the consequences of change with which the Manchus rule the subject people that their customs and prejudices are cherished and perpetuated.

A resolute Chinese chieftain would carry reform as a national sentiment; but after our suicidal course twenty years ago (I mean that it was morally suicidal),—adopted from sheer and short-sighted selfishness, ignoring other causes of distrust as we may, we have no right to expect the confidence of any such patriot. Such an one may arise in the southern half of the country: his advent cannot be expected in the northern;

for, as Lord Elgin wrote when he went to Tientsin in 1858, the pulsation of the national heart is found to decrease as the seat of Government is approached.

In considering the difficulties environing the desiderated emancipation of the people of China from the rusty trammels of a dead past, our attention is arrested by indications of a new national life in Japan whose general aspect is of happy augury for her people ; and to which the critical position of her relations with China lends immediate and special interest: while the new element of this question that so unexpectedly emerges from the Corea, complicates the view presented, whether it may eventually contribute to the more easy solution of it or not.

We are thus brought to the consideration of the relations of China and Japan, and the contrasts presented by reason of their differing politics as affecting their progress, respectively, in assimilation to the civilization of the Western Nations.

The two Empires of Eastern Asia long presented a contrast in their respective politics as marked as it was singular and interesting; and the consequent differing characteristics of the two peoples afford at this day a topic of wondering surprise to the traveller or student who observes their geographical proximity and philological similarities.

China had emancipated herself from the feudal system before the birth of Christ, and substantially adopted that of centralization which exists to-day. Japan, on the contrary, has abolished feudalism only within the present decade. The patriarchal régime in China, although in theory despotic, practically admits essentially democratic elements in administration ; whilst the equality of all men before the Law is a fundamental principle of Government. The people, consequently, exhibit a resolute self-consciousness and a corresponding veneration for the institutions of their ancestors precluding ready accessibility to foreign ideas. The Japanese, on the other hand, bred in feuda-

lism and subject to a peculiar system of caste, are as a people more passively submissive to their Rulers; the seeming qualification of this being only in an occasional excess of zealous patriotism on the part of the military caste.

Hence, to-day there is presented the contrast of Reform by the will of an absolute Ruler imposed upon an ostensibly willing people—on the one hand : and on the other, a Ruler withheld by policy from initiating change among a people held in moral thraldom to the code of ancient observances ;—and while the last constitutes a much more formidable and intricate obstruction of our teaching than the mere will of an Emperor would, it is more deserving of our respect if not even of our confidence.

Japan, the younger nation, that held to the feudal system until yesterday, and in civilization was then to be regarded as an off-shoot of China, is assumed by her Rulers to be prepared for the advanced civilization of Europe; and, on the other hand, China, —that shook off the trammels of feudalism two thousand years ago,—shrinks and trembles at the bare suggestion of the change ! How gratifying the spectacle in Japan if there were no elements of insecurity—no signs of precipitancy—no need of diversions ! Japan renovated—*Europeanised*,—does that mean reformed—regenerated ? Is it possible thus to safely let in a deluge of change ? Is it judicious to attempt it ? We may well doubt it. The hot-house system of forcing is not healthful for even sturdy indigenous plants ; and too many exotics at once may overtask the assimilative properties of the soil.

We see these radical changes applied in Japan under widely different circumstances from what exist in China ; and what is ostensibly possible in Japan, as by authority, is wholly improbable in China: and yet, reasoning from fundamental principles, the Chinese people should be better prepared to encounter the hazard of such changes than the Japanese.

The condition of tutelage in which we now see the Japanese, under the exercise of arbitrary power to compel their immediate adoption of the customs of Europeans, marks, at once, the wide difference between the two ; whereas, on the other hand, the Chinese are deeply grounded in their own national life and have enjoyed for many centuries such a measure of personal, individual freedom as has been accorded the people of Europe only the past two or three centuries,—their Rulers abstaining from interference with their social customs or observances and avoiding even in political affairs a meddling and dictatorial attitude, whilst merely checking attempts against the Dynasty,—the people have been practically much more self-reliant than even the peoples of some European States are at this day. Thus they have been living, so to speak, a constitutional life that has become buttressed about by customs and precedents forming the elements of order and popular authority, to which their military conquerors accord their acquiescence.

Such being the political education engrafted upon the patriarchal system by which the Chinese have been fashioned, let us not deem it strange that, in the consciousness of an ancient and renowned history, they have some national egotism and self-conceit.

On the other hand, we behold the just emancipated child of the feudal system,—an ingenious, but also ingenuous youth ; and we are asked to believe that by one bound from the heavy armor of feudalism— veiled in darkness like that of the middle ages—he can vault into the broad light of the civilization of to day !

We are told by a great philosopher that " *human nature is not a machine to be built after a model, but a tree, which requires to grow and develop itself on all sides, according to the tendency of the inward forces which make it a living thing.*"

Reflecting upon this universal truth, can we, then, believe that the Japanese people, by the simple fiat of their Rulers, can at one stride achieve the position that the people of the more advanced Western Nations have only attained by a course of constitutional training of four or five centuries ? That no period of probation is required for these *disjecta membra* of feudalism to coalesce with the matured offspring of European civilization and Christian reformation ?

Must we not, rather, conclude,—while admitting the virtuous intentions and honorable aspirations of the Rulers and the singular merits of this primitive people of Japan,—that the former are lacking in the profound knowledge of the science of Government which the philosopher, already quoted, plainly indicates as a condition of the proper, healthful, training of such a people ? A training whose first step in Japan would have been the application of a relaxed rule of government in all the relations of life, in order to the inculcation of individual self-reliance. Thus the citizen would become mentally receptive of whatever is worthy of imitation in Western habits and customs.

The Rulers of Japan, therefore, have not yet learnt the first lesson of constitutional Government, which consists in restraining or at least abating their middlesome exercise of power, to give the people scope of volition for the voluntary and consequently gainful adoption of such Western usages, in succession, as are adapted to their gradual progress,—the only sure progress,—toward the higher civilization of Europe and America.

G. NYE.

(To be continued.)

SHORT NOTICES OF NEW BOOKS

AND LITERARY INTELLIGENCE.

Canton and the Bogue.—A Narrative of Six Eventful Months in China. By Walter William Mundy.

The above little work, published by Tinsley, does not pretend to give any exhaustive views upon China affairs. A considerable portion of the book is taken up by a description of the journey and other kindred matters, which, though they are of interest to home readers, will, of course, be of little moment to those in China. A well-merited tribute paid to the Messageries Maritimes steamers for the excellent manner in which they are managed is, however, worthy of note. Mr. Mundy, it may be recollected, was the gentleman who so nearly lost his life in the attack upon the steamer *Spark*, and the chief interest in China will be centred upon the account given of this lamentable affair. Mr. Mundy, among other facts of importance as elucidating the matter, expresses a strong opinion that although the captain was reported to have made a strong resistance he was really attacked in his own cabin, and taken completely by surprise, as Mr. Mundy saw him "only a few minutes after the commencement stretched on the floor of his cabin dead, looking so placid as to make it evident that death had been sudden and without pain." The writer follows up his narrative of the attack by a general disquisition upon pirates in the China Seas, and complains that the Hoppo's gunboats are employed exclusively

* Copies of the works marked thus not having reached us, we quote from home reviews.

in matters of revenue, often to the detriment of our trade in Hong Kong, instead of being actively engaged in hunting out and putting down these pests of the China waters. The volume concludes with a description of the Typhoon of 1874, and some sensible remarks on the present condition of foreigners in China.—*L. & C. Express.*

———

Keramic Art of Japan. Part II. By G. A. Audsley, Architect, and J. A. Bowes, President of the Liverpool Art Club. Liverpool: Published by the Authors for the Subscribers. London: Henry Sotheran and Co.

The second part of this superb work now before us is in every particular fully equal to the first instalment, the appearance of which we hailed with pleasure three months ago. The present part contains pp. xiii. to xxxii. of the Introductory Essay on Japanese Art, together with Plates C, E, and G, illustrating the same; pp. 9 to 12 of Keramic Art of Japan; five very magnificent chromolithographic plates with descriptive letterpress; and two autotype plates, also with descriptions in detail.—*Ibid.*

———

Dr. Anderson, of Calcutta, who was on Colonel Brown's staff, contributes to the current number of *Macmillan's Magazine* an article on "The Exploring Expeditions to Western Yunnan of 1868 and 1875," which, at the present juncture of affairs, will be read with considerable interest. Dr. Anderson warns his readers at starting that they need not dread a discussion of rival trade routes, or an intrusion on the province of diplomacy, his intention being to give briefly an intelligible sketch of Major Sladen's and Colonel Brown's expeditions. This he has done clearly and concisely; but we look in vain for an account or explanation of the crowning catastrophe, the brutal and treacherous outrage on Mr. Margary.— *Ibid.*

A Collection of Chinese Proverbs, translated and arranged by William Scarborough, Wesleyan Missionary, Hankow, 1875.

The 2,700 Proverbs contained in this work form a valuable collection to all who would study the social conditions of the Chinese. If a proverb is rightly described as "the wisdom of many expressed by the wit of one" the volume before us should contain a good deal that is wise. The sayings in question are arranged in 20 sections under distinct headings as follows:—On Agency; on Animals; on Business; on Domestic Concerns; on Education; Facetiæ; on Fortune; on Joys and Sorrows; on Language; on Law and Government; on Man; on Manners; on Medicine; on Morals; on Prudence; the Five Relations; on Religion; on Times; on Travel; on Wealth and Poverty;—besides which there are a number of miscellaneous proverbs. The work is well printed and bound. We refrain from any extended notice, as we hope to notice the work at length in another issue.

The *Chinese Recorder and Missionary Journal* for September-October 1875 opens with a paper by Dr. Bretschneider, on "The Imperial Palace in Peking and the hills and lakes on the Palace Ground." This collection of notes, for it is nothing else, shews considerable research. Hoinos, who has before contributed several articles on Mongolia, contributes one to the present number on "How to travel in Mongolia," which will be useful to Foreigners travelling in the country. Notes on a passage from Yokohama to

Hirosaki follow, and though written in easy style, are not of much interest. The Rev. John W. Davis gives some statistics of the number of Missionaries in China, and their length of residence, &c. His paper might have been made more complete, but is useful as it stands. The Rev. J. S. McIlvaine contributes some very curious speculations on the location of the Garden of Eden, which will doubtless induce criticism. Some notes of a trip to Soochow, various items of Missionary news, and a notice of the second edition of Colonel Yule's Marco Polo, complete the number, which is up to the average.

We are glad to learn that the printing of Dr. Eitel's edition of Williams' Cantonese Dictionary has been commenced. He has decided to insert the Chinese characters for all phrases—a fact which will much gratify intending buyers.

Corpus Christi College, Oxford, says the *Academy*, has made the foundation of the Chinese Chair in the University possible by devoting one of its Fellowships to the purpose.

A fourth and concluding volume of Professor Max Müller's "Chips from a German Workshop," containing essays chiefly on the science of language, will be issued immediately by Messrs. Longman & Co., who are also preparing for publication a work on "The Seventh Great Oriental Monarchy," by Canon Rawlinson.—*Academy.*

Mr. Herbert A. Giles, of H.B.M.'s China Consular Service, has published a work embodying some of his Chinese experience under the title of "Chinese Sketches." A copy has not yet reached us.

Mr. Robert Swinhoe has in an advanced state of preparation, it is stated, an important work on the Birds of China. It will be uniform with Mr. H. E. Dresser's "Birds of Europe," to which it will form, as it may be

termed, a supplement, no species of bird being figured in both. It will consist of about
twenty-eight quarto parts, each part containing about twelve coloured plates, together
with letter-press description of twenty-five
birds.

Mr. Edward Duffield Jones, M.A., late of
the Consular Service in China, has contributed a paper to the *Sunday Magazine*
for October, on "The Chinese: Their Religion and Social Condition."

The Society for the Diffusion of Useful
Knowledge in China has published its third
Report, in which it summarizes the matters
dealt with in the *Peking Magazine* issued
under its auspices. We reproduce them as
a matter of Record. The subjects treated
of include—The rise of Astronomy; Comets;
theory of Eclipses; the transit of Venus, its
theory and uses; the French transit expedition in Peking; Follies of Astrology; Coper-
nicus *versus* Ptolemy; Herschel's Telescope;
the Spectroscope, its history and applica-
tions; views of Meteorology; the Folly of
Fêng-shui. Acoustics; the Telegraph, its
history and operation; Principles of the
Steam Engine. Utility of Railways; the
Engineering of Canals and Rivers—a series;
Suspension Bridges; Diving Apparatus: Gas
and Gas-works; Aeronavigation; English
Agriculture; Manufacture of Glass; Manufacture of Iron; Mr. J. Henderson's Report
on Coal and Iron in Chihli; Photography;
the Calcium Light; the Magic Lantern; Com-
pendium of Geography; Rise of the German
Power. Narrative of a Russian Mission to
the Court of K'anghi; the New Currency of
Japan, with cuts of the Coins; the use of
Paper Money; Postal System of England;
Principles of Life Insurance; the Metric Sys-
tem; Origin of Arabic Numerals; Medical
Jurisprudence; Judicial Torture; the For-
mosan difficulty as a question of Public Law;
Vaccination; Circulation of the Blood; the
Pulse; the Eye. Biographies,—Aristotle;
Archimedes; Harvey; Captain Cook; the

Fables of La Fontaine, etc., etc. A series
of short articles and of miscellaneous facts,
and several columns of news, fill up every
number. There are many papers from Native writers, among whom Professor *Li
Shên-lan*, of the Peking College, is conspicuous.

The foregoing list is most creditable to the
conductors of this periodical, and we regret
to learn that, owing to the difficulty of obtaining contributors, it has been decided to
discontinue it. Efforts are however being
made to get the Chinese Polytechnic Society
at Shanghai to continue it, and these will
we trust be successful.

Messrs. Chapman and Hall will shortly
publish *The Rambles of a Globe-Trotter in
Australia, Japan, China, Java, India, and
Cashmere*, by Mr. E. K. Laird.

An interesting paper on the Straits of Ma-
lacca, from the pen of Commander W. H.
Lewin, appears in the October number of the
Charing Cross Magazine.

Mr. James Jackson Jarves is preparing a
volume entitled *A Glimpse of the Art of
Japan*. It will be illustrated by photolitho-
graphs.

L'Art Khmer. . *Etude Historique sur les
Monuments de l'Ancien Cambodge.*—
Par la Comte de Croizier. Paris: E.
Leroux 1875.
"M. de Croizier divides his modest and
unpretending work into four main parts.
The first part he calls *Etude Historique;* in
Chapter I. he treats of our acquaintance with
Cambodia previous to 1861; Chapter II. is
devoted to the labours of Henri Mouhot,
who, in 1861, discovered afresh the ruins of
the ancient Khmer civilisation, and made
known "the existence of Angkor-Thom, the
ancient capital of the Khmers, and of Ang-
kor-Wat, the Jerusalem of Buddhism."
Chapter III. contains some notes respecting
"*Explorations Diverses;*" and Chapter IV.

an account of Captain de Lagrée's expedition ; with him, it will be remembered, there were associated Lieutenants Garnier and Delaporte, Drs. Thorel and Joubert, and the Vicomte de Carné. Chapter V. reproduces from the *Journal Officiel* the principal passages from the official report of Lieut. Delaporte's subsequent explorations ; and Chapter VI. contains some remarks on the Musée Khmer which has been formed at Compiègne from the specimens of various kinds collected by that industrious officer and other *savants*. In the second part of his work M. de Croizier furnishes a general sketch of the monuments, and describes the materials of which they are composed, the processes of their construction, &c.; and in the third part we have a complete list of the Khmer monuments found up to the present time. The fourth and concluding part contains a detailed catalogue of the contents of the Musée Khmer, which has found a temporary home in the Palace of Compiègne, but which it is intended eventually to transfer to the Louvre. Annexed to this is a map of Southern Indo-China (*ancien royaume* Khmer), on which are indicated by figures the positions in which the various groups of Khmer monuments have been discovered. The volume also contains a portrait of Lieut. Delaporte, together with a few illustrations.—*L. & C. Express.*

The author of the work noticed above has also in preparation for issue by the same firm *Légends Indo-Chinoises, relatives aux Monuments de Pierres, de l'Ancien Cambodge*, and *Premier Recueil d'Inscriptions Khmer, publiées en Europe* (83 *planches*).

NOTES AND QUERIES.

NOTES.

CHINESE JESSAMINE. (Vol. IV., p. 137.) —No Jasmine is indigenous either in the British Isles or in any portion of Northern Europe ; the "English" one referred to by the querist is probably *Jasminum officinale*, Linn., a very old inhabitant of our gardens, truly wild in Western Asia, but now more or less completely naturalised in many parts of Southern Europe; though stated, on the untrustworthy testimony of Loureiro, to be a native of China, there is no reason for believing such to be the case. One of the flowers most commonly employed for scenting Tea is not "misnamed Jessamine," but is a true species of the genus—*J. grandiflorum*, Linn.,—very closely allied to the one above mentioned. These flowers may in summer be seen spread out to dry in large circular bamboo trays, in the more open streets of Canton, and a tea a good deal used at official receptions may be purchased, with which the entire corollas are liberally mixed. To the writer at least, it has a very exciting action on the nerves.

H. F. H.

TORTURE IN BRITISH AND CHINESE PRISONS.—A correspondent writes as follows to the *N. C. D. News*:— The Reviewer of the last number of the *China Review*, writing about Dr. Kerr's paper on *The Prisons of Canton*, says in the *Daily News* to-day :— "But, as the editor of the *Review* remarks, bad as were the practices in our own prisons, there is no evidence to show that such cruelties as making a man kneel for hours on pounded glass, or being slung up by the thumbs or toes, were perpetrated...." and quotes a passage from the article referred to, in which "the fiendish tortures in the days of the Inquisition" do not fail to be once more recalled. It may interest some of your readers to know that the torture of being hung up by one of the limbs is not exclusively Chinese; that the officials of the Inquisition were not a whit more cruel than their victims when the parts were reversed; and that in so civilised a country as England, and during so enlightened an era as the reign of Good (*sic*) Queen Bess, hanging up by the wrists was not unknown. They will have simply to read in the last number of *The Athenæum*, (page 398, September 25th, 1875) the following passage of the Review of Father Morris' new work on *The Troubles of our Catholic Forefathers :—* " ......Weston was arrested as a matter of course, but was fortunate enough to escape the rack and the almost more horrible torture of *being hung up by the wrists*, as John Gerrard, Southwell, and others were a few years afterwards."—[The writer of the foregoing has evidently failed to read the article in question. We referred to an observation in the text that such cruelties were common in our own prisons *less than one hundred years ago.*—ED. C. R.]

FUSANG.—Apropos of our recent Notice of Mr. Leland's *Fusang*, the Rev. J. Goble contributes the following interesting letter to the *Japan Gazette* of Oct. 15 :—

Dear Sir,—I saw in your columns, the other day, a reference to the old question that has so long puzzled many of the antiquarians and *savants* of the western world, viz., "where was Fusang?" I fancy I may be able to give a plausible solution of this ancient problem.

It may be remembered that Prof. Newman and some others have inferred an early discovery of America by the Chinese, and some even go so far as to suppose the ancient Mexicans to be of Chinese origin, because the *Agave Chinensis* (Fusang) is found in Mexico. I do not wish now to discuss either the question, whether the Mexicans are of Chinese origin or the Chinese are of Mexican origin, but intend simply to give my theory of the origin of the doubt and consequent discussion that has been so long

undecided as to the locality or country called *Fusang*.

Some have said that Japan was anciently called by that name, and others have conjectured that ancient *Fusang* must have been somewhere within the borders of the Chinese Empire. I have searched the most ancient native records of Japan, and I think I have found the clue to the unravelling of the ancient mystery. There is an old tradition of a colossal tree called the *Fusao Boku*. This tree was said to have had a trunk several *ri* in diameter, its top reached to heaven and its sheltering branches covered the entire godland (all Japan). When this tree fell then Fujiyama sprang up at the concussion. From this old tradition some ancient writers in China seem to have called Japan *Fusao* or the country of the *Fusao Boku*.

The Chinese characters which in Japan represent the name *Fusao* are pronounced in China *Fusang*.

There is also in Corea on the side of the land most contiguous to Japan a town and harbour called Fusang.

Now, I think that the fact that the names of the *Agave Chinensis* (found in Mexico as well as in China) and the great ancient tree of Japan, and of the port in Corea being the same, is evidently quite sufficient cause for all the doubt and mystery that has so long vexed the western world in reference to the locality of ancient Fusang.

Japan then is the country so long sought under that name, and Mexico has only been accidentally mixed up with China in the mystery, from the fact that each happens to have a tree known to Chinese writers by the same name. Perhaps also the name of the port in Corea has been so called because of the existence there of the Fusang tree (*Agave Chinensis*).

QUERIES.

BELLS.—Have bells ever been hung in belfries by the Chinese? If so, where do such structures exist?   H. A. B.

RED AS A FESTIVE COLOUR.—Can any one explain why red is chosen as a festive colour at marriages, &c., in China? Also, why yellow is the Imperial and white the mourning colour.

ETHNOLOGIST.

THE NATURAL HISTORY OF CHINA.—Will some readers oblige me with notes as to where I can find the best notices in English, French or Latin of what is known respecting Chinese natural history? I have David's travels as published in the *Courier*, and am aware that Mr Swinhoe will shortly publish a work on Chinese ornithology.

NATURALIST.

BOOKS WANTED, EXCHANGES, &c.

(All addresses to care of Editor, China Review.)

BOOKS WANTED.

The undersigned wants a printed or manuscript copy of the following books, 島夷志畧, 安南志畧, 越史畧 and 交州記, the three first of which are mentioned in Wylie's Bibliography respectively on p. 47 and 33. He would feel greatly obliged if any readers of the *China Review* would assist him in procuring these works.

W. P. G.

Li-ki ou Mémorial des Rites, traduit pour la première fois du Chinois et accompagné de notes, de commentaires et du texte original, par J. M. Callery. Turin, 1853.

Address, H. K.

FOR SALE.

Morrison's Dictionary, 6 vols. complete (large edition), price $20.

Address, X.

TO PURCHASE OR EXCHANGE.

Endliches Verzeichniss der Chinesischen und Japanischen Münzen des K. K. Münz, and Antiken-Cabinetes in Wien 1837, 8vo.

Native Treatises on Numismatics.

A Collection of Bank Notes issued by the Daimios of Japan.

Rare Chinese and Japanese Coins.

Address, A.

(Hongkong.)

www.ingramcontent.com/pod-product-compliance
Lightning Source LLC
Chambersburg PA
CBHW020253290326
41930CB00039B/1237